MAKERS
of the
MUSLIM
WORLD

Ibn 'Asakir of Damascus

TITLES IN THE MAKERS OF THE MUSLIM WORLD SERIES

Series Editors: Professor Khaled El-Rouayheb, Harvard University, and Professor Sabine Schmidtke, Institute for Advanced Study, Princeton

For current information and details of other books in the series, please visit oneworld-publications.com/makers-of-the-muslim-world

MAKERS
of the
MUSLIM
WORLD

Ibn 'Asakir of Damascus

Champion of Sunni Islam in the Time of the Crusades

SULEIMAN A. MOURAD

ONEWORLD
ACADEMIC

Oneworld Academic

An imprint of Oneworld Publications

Published by Oneworld Academic in 2021

ISBN 978-0-86154-047-1
eISBN 978-0-86154-046-4

Typeset by Geethik Technologies
Printed and bound in Great Britain by Clays Ltd, Elcograf S.p.A.

Oneworld Publications
10 Bloomsbury Street
London WC1B 3SR
England

Stay up to date with the latest books,
special offers, and exclusive content from
Oneworld with our newsletter

Sign up on our website
oneworld-publications.com

To Dimitri Gutas and Beatrice Gruendler
For their unwavering support and friendship over the years

CONTENTS

NOTES

A few remarks are in order to clarify certain choices I followed in this book. In general, all names are rendered according to the way they are spelled, except in those cases where the person or the place is already very familiar by an Anglicized name, such as Saladin (not Salah al-Din) and Damascus (not Dimashq).

If a person is not familiar in English, I gave their Arabic name, invariably the one they were famous by. This could be *Abu X* (father of X) or *Umm X* (mother of X), or *X b./bt. Y* (X son/daughter of Y), or *Ibn/Bint X* (son/daughter of X). To illustrate: Ibn 'Asakir was known as Abu al-Qasim 'Ali b. al-Hasan al-Dimashqi. Abu al-Qasim was his honorific, 'Ali was his name, al-Hasan was his father's name, and al-Dimashqi meant he was from Damascus. Since he was known by Ibn 'Asakir, I use it throughout to refer to him (even though we do not know exactly why the family came to be known by this nickname and whether or not *'Asakir* was an ancestor). Others, like al-Khatib al-Baghdadi, were known by their profession and place of origin; *al-Khatib* meant the orator, and *al-Baghdadi* meant "the one from Baghdad." Similarly, al-Ash'ari (the one from the Ash'ari clan), Ibn al-Mubarak (son of Mubarak), and so on. This also applied to other communities in the Muslim world in premodern times.

In those cases where I give the name of a person in the form of X son of Y or X daughter of Y, I followed the custom in modern scholarship on Islam to render the Arabic word for son (*ibn*) as b., and for daughter (*bint*) as bt., thus X b. Y if it is a man, and X bt. Y if it is a woman.

For all the students of Ibn 'Asakir, I give their dates of birth as well as their dates of death in order to show the time they could have overlapped with him. I did that as well for all the members of the 'Asakir family to give an idea about the time in which they lived and flourished.

I use Hadith to indicate the entire body of traditions attributed or transmitted on the authority of the Prophet Muhammad and about him. In contrast, I use hadith to refer to an individual anecdote.

The term *Syria* is used throughout the book to designate what is commonly known in late antique and medieval Islamic times as *Bilad al-Sham*. This old Arabic expression originally meant "the Lands to the North," that is north of the Arabian Peninsula. It included the countries today known as Syria (except for the parts to the north and northeast of the Euphrates River, which historically were known as Upper Mesopotamia), Lebanon, Jordan, Palestine, and Israel, and the region of Antioch in Turkey. Therefore, the reader should not understand by *Syria* the current nation-state of Syria.

For dates, I used the Islamic calendar (AH) and the Christian (AD)/ Common Era (CE) calendar dating systems. The former is given first followed by the latter: e.g., Ibn 'Asakir was born in 499/1105, where 499 refers to the Islamic year, and 1105 to the AD/CE year.

And finally, for difficult concepts or names, I provide a Glossary at the end of the book. The first time I mention one of these terms, it is marked by an asterisk (*) to indicate that it is explained there.

ACKNOWLEDGMENTS

I have been working on the scholarship of Ibn 'Asakir for around thirty years. This book benefits directly or indirectly from this long exposure to him and the help I have received during this time from countless institutions and people, too many to list here. I am especially thankful for the generous feedback colleagues have shared with me in several venues, be it at conferences and workshops, or even by reading some of my books and articles on Ibn 'Asakir and sending me comments and suggestions. Without this collective wisdom, my thinking of Ibn 'Asakir would not have evolved to the level of writing a book on him and about his contribution to Islamic scholarship and intellectual history.

A work like this one requires a lot of resources and support. I was able to finish it during my sabbatical year 2019–2020 from Smith College. I am thankful to the generous sabbatical support that the College provides. Moreover, some of the research, specifically for Chapter 7, benefitted from a generous grant from the Gerda Henkel Stiftung (Germany).

I would also like to thank my friend Khaled El-Rouayheb and the editorial team of Oneworld's Makers of the Muslim World series, for publishing this volume on Ibn 'Asakir and also for valuable guidance and recommendations. I am equally thankful to the anonymous reviewers for their significant feedback and suggestions, and to my friend and colleague James E. Lindsay (another aficionado of Ibn 'Asakir) for reading the manuscript and sharing with me some very insightful suggestions.

I am also grateful for the magical fingers and entrancing voices of many West African and Cuban musicians whose inspirational tunes accompanied the writing of this book, and created a stimulating atmosphere for the ideas to flow.

1

THE WORLD OF IBN 'ASAKIR

'Ali Ibn 'Asakir was a towering figure in medieval Islamic scholarship. Due mostly to his influence and aura, the family became a prominent Sunni* household in medieval Damascus, producing a large number of notable Shafi'i* scholars, both men and women, who occupied prestigious scholarly, judicial, and administrative positions in Syria and Egypt, and who helped shape the intellectual and religious life there, especially between the fifth/eleventh and eighth/fourteenth centuries. Even though each member of the family was known as Ibn 'Asakir along with a peculiar honorific, the reference on its own in medieval literature invariably refers to him and thus signifies his eminence within the family.

Ibn 'Asakir's impact can be measured along three aspects. First, his writings – on Islamic religious history, on Hadith*, and on religious merits of several towns and locales in and around Damascus – had a tremendous influence on later scholars. Second, his advocacy and teaching of major books – e.g., *Sahih* of al-Bukhari, *Sahih* of Muslim, *al-Tabaqat al-kubra* of Ibn Sa'd, *Kitab al-Jihad* of Ibn al-Mubarak – played a fundamental role in the dissemination of these books and the revival of Sunnism, more accurately a particular form of Sunnism in Syria and Egypt that became dominant among the scholarly elites. Third, his political advocacy and religious propaganda against Shi'is* and Franks (Crusaders) were part of a broader current that helped some Muslim rulers – especially Nur al-Din (d. 569/1174) and Saladin (d. 589/1193) – secure the allegiance of a large sector of the Sunni scholarly establishment in Syria and Egypt, and launch the revivification of Sunnism there. Each of these aspects was a key building block in the

gradual transformation of the Levant into a majority Sunni region and
the maintenance of Sunnism's dominance there to the present day.

DAMASCUS IN THE FIFTH/ELEVENTH CENTURY

It is very important to know the world into which Ibn 'Asakir was
born. It does not only help us understand the necessary context, but
more importantly it is essential for grasping the specific trajectory
of Ibn 'Asakir's life and career, and his subsequent legacy in Islamic
scholarship. For what unfolded in the fifth/eleventh century created
the kind of conditions that allowed scholars like Ibn 'Asakir to emerge
and play a unique role in the history of Damascus and Syria, and by
extension in Islamic religious thought.

The conditions of the time also gave rise to an aspiration among
the Sunni scholarly community in Syria, and among some of the Sunni
masses as well, for a political patron to sponsor a Sunni revival and put
an end to what is known as the "Shi'i Century." During the fourth/
tenth and fifth/eleventh centuries, Syria was ruled by Shi'i dynasties. The Fatimids* (296/909–566/1171), who were based in Egypt
starting in 358/969, controlled central and southern Syria, especially
Palestine, the region of Damascus, and the coast. The Hamdanids
(332/944–394/1004), who at one point ruled Aleppo and Mosul
and the regions between them as well as parts of Upper Mesopotamia
(al-Jazira*), were replaced at the beginning of the fifth/eleventh
century in Aleppo with another Shi'i dynasty called the Mirdasids
(415/1025–472/1080).

The political hegemony of Shi'ism in Damascus and broadly in Syria
meant that the Sunnis there not only had to put up with Shi'i political
dominance but, even worse, with what they considered Shi'i religious
heresies. Moreover, they lacked the economic resources to sponsor
their own institutions as Sunnis in the eastern parts of the Muslim
world were able to do at the time.

With respect to Damascus and Syria more broadly, one should be
mindful of the importance of their history, or to put it more correctly,

their historical memory. Damascus was once the capital of the Islamic empire under the Umayyad* dynasty (40/661–132/750); even in years when an Umayyad Caliph moved his court to a different city (e.g., al-Rasafa to the southeast of Aleppo), Damascus remained the political capital. As such, the Damascenes always looked back to that time – and they still do – as the golden age of their city, and aspired for that golden age to return some day.

Damascus, therefore, was a very different city in the fifth/eleventh century than the sixth/twelfth century when Ibn ʿAsakir lived and became active as a scholar. Syria, too, was a very different region. As noted above, for most of the fifth/eleventh century, political power was in the hands of the Shiʿi Fatimids, whose contentious rule over central and southern Syria witnessed a great deal of resistance from other Shiʿi tribes there. The rule of the Shiʿi Mirdasids, who emerged from the ashes of the Hamdanids and controlled the city of Aleppo and its region, was equally turbulent; they often ran their affairs as vassals either for the Fatimid Caliphate or of the Byzantine Empire. The period also witnessed a revival in the military power of the Byzantines, allowing them to return to the Syrian scene, especially in the northwest. Moreover, Syria at the time had a large Christian community, which was divided into several denominations whose main concentration was in the cities and rural villages to the west and in Upper Mesopotamia. There was also a significant presence of different sects of Shiʿism in and around the major cities. For instance, the main tribe that controlled the countryside and desert in northern Syria was the Shiʿi Banu Kilab confederation, to which the Mirdasids belonged. Central Syria, including the regions outside Damascus, was populated by the Kalb tribal confederation, who were also Shiʿis. Palestine featured the presence of a third major Shiʿi tribe called the Banu Tayy.

Damascus itself remained the largest Sunni city in Syria. But the absence of political stability created a grim reality in the town. Powerful local gangs imposed themselves on the local society, further exacerbating the fears of the Sunni scholarly elites as they watched the significance of their city deteriorate and their status wane among their Sunni counterparts in Iraq and farther east.

Then during the 1070s and 1080s, the Sunni Seljuks* overran all of Syria and toppled the Shiʻi dynasties there. The Fatimids retrenched to Egypt (though they kept control of most of the Syrian coast), and the other dynasties folded. The Seljuk conquests marked the political downfall of Shiʻism in Syria. It also marked the beginning of a demographic change as Sunni Turkic and Kurdish tribes started to settle in large numbers there. It did not, however, mean a swift resurgence of Sunnism. The Seljuk chiefs in Syria split the cities among themselves and competed for political dominance. Unlike Iran and Iraq, which were for the most part under the direct control of the Seljuk Sultan, Syria was only nominally so. Damascus changed hands several times, as Seljuk warlords vied with one another for control of the city, until it finally came under the rule of the Burids, who offered a modicum of stability. The first Burid ruler was Tughtakin (r. 497/1104–522/1128), followed by his son Buri (r. 522/1128–526/1132), then Buri's three sons Ismaʻil (r. 526/1132–529/1135), Mahmud (r. 529/1135–533/1139), and Muhammad (533/1139–534/1140), and finally Muhammad's son Abaq (534/1140–549/1154).

The Burids

The Burid dynasty restored to Damascus and central Syria a degree of political stability. More importantly, they were able to offer the Sunni scholarly establishment an assurance that their long subordination to Shiʻi rule had finally come to an end. But the Burids were not always efficient in maintaining calm. For instance, in summer 523/1129, Sunni mobs massacred many local Nizari Ismaʻilis*, which created an atmosphere of fear in the city and brought back the anxieties of the previous century. This only intensified the desire among the Sunni scholarly establishment for a strong ruler who could put an end to the mayhem and insecurity and make way for the resurgence of Sunnism.

Another important contribution that the Burids made in Damascus, and which had a positive impact on the Sunni scholarly community, was the gradual increase in professorships and patronage of Sunni scholarly activities in the city. The first college (madrasa*) of Islamic law in the city was established under the Burids' predecessors in 491/1098. It

was called the Sadiriyya College, named after the Seljuk officer Shuja'
al-Dawla Sadir b. 'Abd Allah. It specialized in Hanafi* law which,
ironically, while it was the school of choice among the Seljuks, did
not have any significant followers in Damascus. Consequently, the
Sadiriyya College had a lackluster influence on the city. But shortly
thereafter in 514/1120, another college, this one for Shafi'i law, was
founded: the Aminiyya College, named after its benefactor Amin
al-Dawla Kumashtakin (d. 541/1146), who was chief of the army
under Tughtakin and Mahmud, and who also became governor of
Busra and Sarkhad (in the Hawran region, south of Damascus). Its first
professor was one of Ibn 'Asakir's teachers: Abu al-Hasan al-Sulami
(d. 533/1139). Because it specialized in Shafi'i law, many Damascenes
referred to it as the first school in Damascus, which is only correct in
the sense that, unlike the Sadiriyya College, the Aminiyya College was
the first school that really resonated with the majority of the Sunnis in
the city on scholarly and practical levels. Hence the popular sentiment
about the importance of the Burids.

Several other colleges were built by members of the Burid administration, such as the Hanbaliyya College endowed by scholar and Burid
courtier 'Abd al-Wahhab b. 'Abd al-Wahid al-Hanbali (d. 536/1141)
as a school for Hanbali* law, the Mujahidiyya College, built by the senior
Burid army commander Mujahid al-Din Bazzan (d. 555/1160), and
the Mu'iniyya College, built in 524/1130 by the Burid general Mu'in
al-Din Unur (d. 544/1149) – who later became the vizier of Abaq and
the de facto ruler of Damascus between 534/1140–544/1149.

A short explanation of the significance and transformative impact of
colleges at the time is in order. Colleges were important for practical
as well as scholarly reasons. They trained jurists, judges, secretaries,
scribes, etc., who went on to occupy various administrative and judicial roles in their city and society. These roles included running the
courts (each branch of jurisprudence had its legal theory and practical application), providing legal advice to rulers and commanders,
inspecting and organizing the markets, collecting taxes, overseeing
the treatment and rights of non-Muslims, attending to marriage con-
tracts and divorces, settling inheritance cases, and so on. Colleges
also produced an academic and scholarly cadre who would assure the

continuation of its educational mission. Equally important is that, given the interdependence of several fields of study, they necessitated the active teaching of related fields, which were essential for the study of the main topic of teaching at a given college. Therefore, the study of Shafiʿi law at the Aminiyya College, for example, required certain expertise in a number of related areas. So even though there was one professor who occupied the chair of teaching Shafiʿi law at the Aminiyya College, the students were expected to also study Arabic language, the Qurʾan and its exegesis, Hadith and its sciences, Islamic history, other branches of jurisprudence, theology, and so on. These topics were taught either at other colleges or in other religious centers around town, such as the Umayyad Mosque, where students learned subjects, especially Arabic language and Islamic history, that were not the focus of any one institution. Therefore, colleges generated a boost in scholarly and intellectual life, which led to a renaissance in learning around the city. They also created many forms of employment, such as endowment managers, and custodians.

Moreover, colleges had a very important political impact, especially in terms of fostering a symbiotic relationship between rulers and scholars in many cities across the Muslim world at the time. Endowing a college gave the rulers (and members of their household or court) the chance to demonstrate their religious bona fides and piety. The scholars received employment and expanded their influence and wealth. In return, they gave the rulers, most of the time at least, their political support and acquiescence, which enhanced the rulers' prestige in the city.

The Seljuk domination in Syria, which many Sunnis saw as their deliverance from the yoke of Shiʿism, was shattered when the Crusaders arrived on the scene in 490/1097 and captured cities such as Edessa, Antioch, Maʿarrat al-Nuʿman and, ultimately, Jerusalem in July 1099. In the next twenty-five years, the Franks (as they were collectively referred to by the Muslims) were able to add to their gains and establish control of the entire coastline. One of the consequences of the Crusader invasion was the relocation of a large number of Sunni scholars, particularly from coastal towns and Palestine to Damascus. Some of them were of very good caliber and were appointed as mosque imams in several locations in and around the city. One of their major contributions was transforming their mosques into centers of education, thus enriching the teaching and scholarly output of the city, especially in Hadith.

Seljuk-Crusader relations were a mix of war and peace. The various warlords on both sides prioritized their individual interests. Thus, many Seljuk chiefs in Syria concluded truces with the Franks or oscillated between war and peace with them. The Burids oscillated between the two strategies, but gradually, and with time, they hammered out an alliance with the Kingdom of Jerusalem, which irked some of the local Damascene Sunni scholars who were of the opinion that the only way to deal with the invading Franks was through jihad. Among the confrontationists were a vocal group of the displaced scholars from Palestine and coastal Syria, some of whom Ibn 'Asakir knew very well as a child. They advocated jihad and pushed their fellow Damascenes to pressure the Burids whenever they concluded a truce or an alliance with the Franks.

The Burids did not abandon their strategy, however. They were more concerned with the threats posed to them from powerful Muslim foes. In other words, they felt they were caught between a rock and a hard place. To the south and west were the Crusaders, and to the north were fellow Seljuk chieftains who had their own designs on Damascus. One of those warlords was the Seljuk prince 'Imad al-Din Zangi (d. 541/1146), who in the late 1120s gained control of the city of Mosul in northern Iraq, Aleppo, and most of the area between them. In 539/1144, he captured Edessa from the Crusaders, which instantly transformed him into one of Islam's greatest heroes; the capture of Edessa was hailed as the first major accomplishment that turned the tide in favor of the Muslims in northern Syria and Upper Mesopotamia. Upon Zangi's death, his eldest son Sayf al-Din (d. 544/1149) inherited what everyone then thought was the more prestigious Mosul. Zangi's other son, Nur al-Din, took over in Aleppo, a city rife with problems and a large population of Shi'is.

Both brothers coveted Damascus yet, publicly at least, Nur al-Din supported his brother given the latter's seniority and power. The Burids were very concerned about the brothers' ambitions. Mu'in

al-Din Unur, who actually administered the city during the reign of
the Burid ruler Abaq, was very pragmatic in his political choices: he
believed that Damascus should play the Franks and the Zangids against
each other. He thus forged simultaneous alliances with Nur al-Din (by
marrying him to his daughter) and with the Franks.

Things were thrown into turmoil when the Crusaders attacked
Damascus in the early summer of 543/1148. This undermined the
Burids' policy of peace towards the Franks and exposed them to serious criticism from the Sunni religious establishment. It did not matter
that the Franks' short siege failed utterly and the threat to the Burids
had faded away. The damage was done. It pushed the Sunni scholarly
elites to reassess whether their city needed a new ruler to protect it;
some were open, some even very eager, for Nur al-Din to be that
ruler.

Nur al-Din

The death of Unur in August 544/1149, followed shortly by that of
Sayf al-Din in November, presented Nur al-Din with an extraordinary opportunity to assume leadership of the Zangid state and capture
Damascus. He knew that in order to achieve the former he needed
the latter, for only the city of Damascus could provide him with an
effective counter to the much richer Mosul. Nur al-Din moved against
and laid siege to Damascus twice, but each time the Burids were able
to repel his advances. In the meantime, he dispatched to Damascus
his advisor, the jurist Burhan al-Din al-Balkhi (d. 548/1153), to
sway the scholarly establishment to support his takeover of the city.
Burhan al-Din was originally from Balkh and made a name for himself as an authority on Hanafi law. Nur al-Din had appointed him in
543/1148 as professor of Hanafi law at the Halawiyyun College in
Aleppo (which was initially a Shi'i school). He also tasked him with
the job of supervising the religious reforms there, which necessitated
a systematic "cleansing" of Shi'i practices and rituals, and replacing
them with Sunni ones, as well as the confiscation of Shi'i schools,
mosques, and other religious infrastructure and turning them into
Sunni institutions.

Burhan al-Din al-Balkhi knew Damascus well and had excellent contacts with many scholars there, who agitated for him to become the professor of Hanafi law at the Sadiriyya College on account of his great expertise in Islamic jurisprudence. When the Burids became suspicious of his activities, they expelled him from the city, but eventually allowed him to return at the insistence of the local scholarly elites. Under the cover of scholarship, he made sure to endear his patron Nur al-Din to the Sunni establishment in Damascus. When Nur al-Din once again sought to capture Damascus – third time is a charm, as the adage goes – they were ready to welcome him. In April 549/1154, Abaq, the last Burid ruler of Damascus, had no choice but to hand over the city to Nur al-Din, who compensated him with Hims. Burhan al-Din's plan was a rousing success, but unfortunately for him he died on 29 Sha'ban 548/19 November 1153, five months before the city surrendered to Nur al-Din.

Damascus was very different to Aleppo. It did not require much "cleansing" of Shi'i religious practices. Nevertheless, Nur al-Din realized the city badly needed more religious institutions and hospitals in order to be a true capital. The Sunnification drive he had launched in Aleppo was applied as well in Damascus, but with some important differences. Damascus did not have an existing network of Shi'i schools to confiscate, so Nur al-Din had to build them from scratch (although he did confiscate some residential housing). He, members of his family and his local officials engaged in a kind of competition of endowing schools, Sufi dwellings, infirmaries, and many other public and administrative buildings that transformed the social landscape in Syria. One example is the first college for the study of Hadith, which Nur al-Din endowed in the 560s/1160s for Ibn 'Asakir (see Chapter 3).

This systematic effort in Damascus, Aleppo, and other cities – which Nur al-Din's Ayyubid successors continued – launched a renaissance that lasted several centuries and resulted in the transformation of Syria into a powerhouse of Sunni scholarship. In the particular case of Damascus, this network of prestigious schools gave the city's scholars a huge boost and catapulted them within a short period to a position of prominence in the Muslim world. For the first time ever, students from other cities started to flock to Damascus to study with its scholars, whose books and writings on different topics of Islamic religious thought became a hot commodity. Many professors as well were lured to Damascus on account of the well-endowed network of colleges. (One should add that the growing frequency of Mongol raids and the ultimate invasion in the course of the seventh/thirteenth century decimated many Sunni centers of scholarship in the Muslim east, and also helped shift the tide in favor of Syria and Egypt.)

This helps us understand why Sunni scholars all over Syria at the time idolized Nur al-Din during his lifetime, assuring the Sultan a unique legacy in Sunni history and genealogy. What also endeared him to them was the great respect and deference he showed them. We know of many stories about Nur al-Din attending classes with scholars in Aleppo and Damascus, including several seminars with Ibn 'Asakir (see Chapter 3). He also encouraged them and even asked them specifically to write books for him; for example, he commissioned both Ibn 'Asakir and another jurist from Aleppo named Majd al-Din Ibn Jahbal (d. 596/1200) to compile books on jihad. In other words, the Sultan not only knew how to win them over with endowed professorships and colleges, but he actively involved some of them (for example, Burhan al-Din, Ibn 'Asakir, Majd al-Din) in his political project.

Nevertheless, one has to realize that Nur al-Din's overture to the Sunni scholars in Syria was partly pragmatic: to assure their support, allegiance and service for his ambition to unify Syria, and to use the strength of that unity to wrest Egypt from the Fatimid Caliphs. For such an ambitious project, he needed the populace to support him and rally behind him, and not around his Muslim rivals. To achieve this objective, it was necessary to win over the scholars so that they could do his bidding in their respective communities.

As for his relations with the Franks, Nur al-Din adopted the same policy as that of the Burids: a mix of war and peace. But the scholars did not want to believe that he was a shrewd politician who was guided by pragmatism. They only wanted to believe that he was determined to lead a jihad campaign – hence their nickname for him, *al-malik al-mujahid* (the jihad warrior monarch) – whose urgent priority was to drive out the Franks and to liberate Jerusalem. Nur al-Din, however, was far too astute to fall for that, knowing full well that a successful all-out confrontation with the Franks was impossible in the short term, though it certainly could be a long-term goal.

Status of Religious Scholarship

As explained above, even though the majority of Muslims in Damascus in the fifth/eleventh century were Sunnis, they lacked what other major cities had in terms of schools, infrastructure, and sponsorship, which limited Damascene Sunni scholars' visibility and impact compared to their colleagues elsewhere. Their scholarly networks were weak, and centers for religious knowledge were limited or nonexistent. The longing for scholars of high caliber in their city can be seen in how they came to remember the visits of three important Sunni scholars during the course of the second half of the fifth/eleventh century: al-Khatib al-Baghdadi, Nasr al-Maqdisi, and Abu Hamid al-Ghazali. Their respective sojourns in Damascus illustrate the humble level of religious scholarships in the city and the eagerness of local scholars to raise their profile among their Sunni counterparts in other regions.

Al-Khatib al-Baghdadi (d. 463/1071) was one of Baghdad's celebrated scholars, who became known for his monumental biographical encyclopedia on the city. Popularly called *Ta'rikh Baghdad* (*History of Baghdad*), it was the book that inspired Ibn 'Asakir to write his own *Ta'rikh Dimashq* (see Chapter 4). Al-Khatib al-Baghdadi was an expert on Hadith scholarship, and composed several works on the writing and transmission of Hadith. He was also famed for his anti-Hanbali and anti-Shi'i rants, earning him the animosity of both groups.

In 451/1059, al-Khatib al-Baghdadi came to Damascus after fleeing political disturbances in his hometown, and stayed there until early 459/1067. During this time, he regularly lectured in the Umayyad Mosque, sometimes on topics that irritated both Hanbalis and Shi'is. Damascus was then under Shi'i Fatimid rule, and al-Khatib al-Baghdadi's religious activism was a matter of concern for the local governor and Shi'i elites. They ultimately expelled him from the city; the official pretext they used to chase him out was an affair al-Khatib al-Baghdadi had with a local boy.

Nasr b. Ibrahim al-Maqdisi (d. 490 /1096) was a notable Hadith scholar from Nablus in Palestine. He spent his early career in Jerusalem and Tyre. In 480/1087, he came to Damascus and stayed there until his death. Upon his arrival, and because of his expertise, he became the leader of the Shafi'is in the city and an authority on Islamic law. His main teaching was held in the courtyard of the Umayyad Mosque, under the archway in the northwestern corner; the place came to be known after him as the *Zawiya** of Nasr al-Maqdisi.

Abu Hamid al-Ghazali (d. 505/1111) was one of the most celebrated scholars of Sunni Islam. He was primarily a theologian whose main contribution was the normalization of the practices and beliefs of Sufism within mainstream Sunni Islam; his central argument was that Sufism is sanctioned by the Qur'an and the Sunna* of Muhammad. He also was an expert in Islamic law. In 484/1091, he was appointed professor at the new and most prestigious school at the time: the Nizamiyya College in Baghdad. In late 488/1095, he left Baghdad for Syria intending a spiritual retreat in Jerusalem. He stopped in Damascus for a few days on his way there, returning to the city at the end of 489/1096. His second residency in Damascus lasted around two years, not the ten years as alleged by al-Dhahabi (d. 748/1348), who attributed his assertion to Ibn 'Asakir; however, there is no mention of this in any of Ibn 'Asakir's known works. In the course of this period, al-Ghazali taught in the *Zawiya* of Nasr al-Maqdisi, whom he knew well. It was during this sojourn that al-Ghazali finished his infamous book *Ihya' 'ulum al-din (Revivification of the Religious Sciences)*.

We do not know much about al-Ghazali's own opinion of the Damascenes or his visit there. But we do know what the Sunni Damascenes thought of him. Initially, he was dismissed by the Sufis and the scholarly establishment on account of his poor dress. But once they realized the depth of his knowledge and discovered who he was, he became a sensation and local scholars as well as students flocked to learn from him. They also circulated many stories about his visit and activities that read more like legends than as history. For instance, one story speaks of him entering the Aminiyya College and discovering that the teacher there was lecturing on one of his books. The problem is that the Aminiyya College did not as yet exist; as said earlier it was founded nine years after al-Ghazali's death, not to mention more than two decades after he left Damascus.

Despite the questionable nature of these legends, they still provide us with valuable information about the way the Damascenes remembered and venerated al-Ghazali. Moreover, the fact that they renamed the *Zawiya* of Nasr al-Maqdisi in the northwestern corner of the Umayyad Mosque courtyard the *Zawiya* of al-Ghazali underscores their reverence for him, especially given the fact that they also revered Nasr al-Maqdisi. (The two designations have been used interchangeably ever since.)

Leaving aside the issue of historical accuracy, the way the Sunni Damascene scholars came to remember the residencies of these three exceptional figures demonstrates that they considered them among the greatest highlights of the city's history at that time. They did so precisely because their sojourns occurred in a specific troubling period, when Sunnis there were cognizant of their desperate need for this caliber of scholarly expertise in their city. The three scholars brought to Damascus an exceptional proficiency in Hadith (this was especially the case of al-Khatib al-Baghdadi and Nasr al-Maqdisi) and knowledge of law and theology that pointed the locals towards a particular form of Sunnism and, more importantly, to the necessary corpus of sources that they should master in order to attain expertise in it. In other words, they charted the nature and trajectory of Sunnism in Damascus and by extension in the Muslim world thereafter, especially in light of the role that Damascus came to play in the revivification of Sunnism in Syria and Egypt starting in the sixth/twelfth century.

It is not an exaggeration to say that every notable Damascene teacher of Ibn 'Asakir studied with these three scholars and accompanied them during their respective sojourns in the city. Moreover, Ibn 'Asakir transmitted countless hadiths and anecdotes from al-Khatib al-Baghdadi, Nasr al-Maqdisi and al-Ghazali via his own teachers, which attests to the importance he and his teachers ascribed to them.

It is very important to add as well that al-Khatib al-Baghdadi, Nasr al-Maqdisi, and al-Ghazali were Ash'aris* in their theological persuasion and Shafi'is in their legal affiliation. Therefore, the boost that they gave to these two scholarly traditions in Damascus was transformative among fellow Shafi'is and Ash'aris, more so than among members of other Sunni sects.

BACK TO IBN 'ASAKIR

Ibn 'Asakir was born into and grew up in an environment saturated with high expectations, fears and desires, uncertainties and promises. His teachers longed for their city to be like Nishapur, Isfahan, and Baghdad, teaming with Sunni colleges, professors, and students, and taking the lead in the revival of Sunnism in Syria and the Muslim world. They aspired to see Damascus restored as a capital city as in the days of yore. They imparted all of these expectations to Ibn 'Asakir and his generation, and drove them to seek knowledge and bring it back to Damascus and make the dream a reality.

Clearly, Ibn 'Asakir was made for this task. He imbibed these hopes and worked his entire life to realize this dream. He idolized the likes of al-Khatib al-Baghdadi, Nasr al-Maqdisi, and al-Ghazali and was determined to follow in their footsteps, even surpass them. He wanted to make them proud of the legacy they left behind in Damascus. He also believed that God had selected Nur al-Din for a task unique in Islamic history. He placed himself in the service of the Sultan, ready to provide the scholarly advice and propaganda necessary to achieve the goal of the unification of Syria and Egypt and the revivification of Sunnism in both.

2

LIFE AND CAREER

BACKGROUND

Abu al-Qasim 'Ali b. al-Hasan, famously known as Ibn 'Asakir, was born in Damascus in Muharram 499/September 1105. He hails from a family about which we know almost nothing prior to his father. Specifically, we do not know anything about the name *'Asakir* for which he and all the members of the family came to be known. It was reported that during his life, he hated to be referred to as Ibn 'Asakir, insisting that people should call him Abu al-Qasim.

His father Abu Muhammad al-Hasan b. Hibat Allah (460/1068–519/1125) was a certified notary in the city. Like many educated Sunni elites at the time, he was also interested in Hadith scholarship, and even though he did not excel in it, he developed close friendships with many of those who did. Aside from that, we know nothing about al-Hasan or his origin except that he had a brother.

Ibn 'Asakir's mother, known only by her honorific "Umm al-Qasim," was the daughter of Abu al-Mufaddal Yahya b. 'Ali al-Qurashi (444/1051–534/1139), the chief-judge of Damascus, and sister of Abu al-Ma'ali Muhammad b. Yahya al-Qurashi (467/1074–537/1142) who followed his father in that post. This connection to one of the most prestigious families of Damascus, which traced its origin to the Umayyad dynasty and thus to Quraysh*, gave Ibn 'Asakir and his siblings certain advantages and facilitated their access to the scholarly elites, positioning them well for prestigious careers and social prominence.

Ibn 'Asakir had two brothers and a sister. The elder brother, Hibat Allah, was a notable scholar of law, Hadith, and Qur'an. He was born

in 488/1095, and first studied in Damascus, then embarked on an
extensive educational journey to Iraq and the eastern Muslim world,
which lasted for four years (510/1116–514/1120). Upon his return
to Damascus, he became the teaching assistant of his old professor
Abu al-Hasan 'Ali b. al-Musallam al-Sulami (d. 533/1139), the most
notable local scholar of Shafi'i law at the time. In fact, al-Sulami had
recently been appointed to the inaugural professorship at the Aminiyya
College, which was established in 514/1120 as the first school for
Shafi'i jurisprudence in Damascus. Hibat Allah also taught Hadith and
law at the *Zawiya* of al-Ghazali located in the northwestern corner
of the inner courtyard of the Umayyad Mosque, and which, as mentioned in Chapter 1, was named after the famous al-Ghazali who used
to teach there during his sojourns in Damascus. Hibat Allah was also
offered the oratory post in the Umayyad Mosque but turned it down,
and even declined the position of deputy chief-judge of the city, opting
instead to dedicate his life to learning and teaching. Thus, he was nicknamed *sa'in al-din* (or simply *al-sa'in*), meaning the one who preserves
the religion of Islam. He died in 563/1168 as a result of a fall which
left him paralyzed for a few days. His role in Ibn 'Asakir's intellectual
formation was immense.

Ibn 'Asakir's younger brother, Muhammad, was born shortly after
the year 500/1107. Following his education in Damascus, he became
a local judge. He was not known for any scholarly achievements and
did not reach the prominence of his two older siblings, but it was his
sons, grandchildren, and great-grandchildren who continued the legacy of the 'Asakir family in the scholarly life of greater Syria and also
Egypt in the thirteenth and fourteenth centuries (see Chapter 5). He
died in 565/1170.

Ibn 'Asakir also had a sister who was married to Abu Bakr
Muhammad b. 'Ali al-Sulami (d. 564/1169) from the notable Sulami
family of Damascus. Abu Bakr al-Sulami became the chief orator of the
Umayyad Mosque and inherited the professorship of Shafi'i law at the
Aminiyya College after his father Abu al-Hasan al-Sulami.

As this indicates, and as we will see subsequently, family connec-
tions, especially through marriage, and teacher-disciple relationships
were very important factors in helping the members of the 'Asakir

family ascend the social and professional ladders in Damascus. This was a time when the scholarly community was small, unlike what it would become later in the sixth/twelfth century and thereafter. Therefore, to have one's grandfather or uncle, or even brother-in-law in key scholarly or professional positions in the city could well be the difference between an average education followed by a mediocre career and an education with more prestigious professors, followed by a guaranteed teaching post at the Umayyad Mosque or one of the first colleges in the city.

EDUCATION AND TRAVELS

Ibn 'Asakir began his pursuit of religious scholarship at a very early age. His elder brother, Hibat Allah, played a defining role in this respect, taking him to meet and study with some of the prominent scholars of Damascus, and later charting his academic itinerary when Ibn 'Asakir travelled for his education. We are told that in 505/1111, at six years of age, Hibat Allah brought his younger sibling to study Hadith with Abu al-Wahsh Subay' b. al-Musallam (d. 508/1115). He also took him to study with Abu Turab Haydara b. Ahmad al-Ansari (d. 506/1112) who, in addition to Hadith, taught Ibn 'Asakir a volume of the *Ta'rikh Baghdad* by al-Khatib al-Baghdadi. Both scholars also trained him in poetry. Hibat Allah then brought him to learn Hadith with Qawwam b. Zayd al-Murri (d. 509/1116). In 507/1113, at age eight, Ibn 'Asakir studied Hadith with another prominent local scholar named Abu al-Qasim 'Ali b. Ibrahim al-Nasib al-Husayni (d. 508/1114), who was originally a Shi'i and converted to Sunnism. Abu al-Qasim al-Nasib, along with Abu al-Hasan 'Ali b. al-Hasan al-Mawazini (d. 514/1120), gave Ibn 'Asakir a certificate (*ijaza**) to transmit the *Tafsir al-qur'an* (*Exegesis of the Qur'an*) of 'Abd al-Razzaq al-San'ani (d. 211/827), and taught him the *Kitab al-Mujalasa* (*On Social Interaction*) of Abu Bakr al-Dinawari (d. after 332/944).

Ibn 'Asakir also learned the Qur'an and its sciences with Abu al-Fath Nasr b. al-Qasim al-Maqdisi (d. 539/1145) and with the blind reciter Abu al-Tammam Kamil b. Ahmad (540/1146). He trained in

Shafi'i law with Abu al-Hasan al-Sulami, first in the *Zawiya* of Ghazali, and later in the Aminiyya College. His own maternal grandfather Abu al-Mufaddal Yahya tutored him in the sciences of the Arabic language and Islamic law, and his elder brother Hibat Allah introduced him to some of the major sources of Hadith: *al-Tabaqat al-kubra* (*Great Generations*) of Ibn Sa'd (d. 230/845) and the *Sunan* (*Prophetic Traditions*) of al-Daraqutni (d. 385/995). Abu al-Qasim Ahmad b. Muhammad al-Hashimi (d. 534/1139) taught him the *Muwatta'* (*The Trodden Path*) of 'Abd Allah b. Wahb (d. 197/813).

Indeed, Hadith was Ibn 'Asakir's main field of interest as a student, and beside the collections of Hadith, he also developed an expertise in its sciences and its transmitters – the proper spelling of their names, education and travels, dates of birth and death, distinguishing them from others who share similar names, their trustworthiness, etc. These were important issues for Hadith scholarship because they allowed for the determination of the soundness of hadiths by verifying the validity of the chains of transmission that allegedly passed them from the Prophet Muhammad and his Companions* down through the centuries. For instance, with Abu Muhammad 'Abd al-Karim b. Hamza al-Sulami (d. 526/1132) Ibn 'Asakir studied *Kitab al-Ikmal* (*The Complete Book*) of Ibn Makula (d. c. 485/1092), as well as *Ta'rikh mawlid al-'ulama' wa-wafayatihim* (*History of the Birth-dates of Hadith Scholars and their Death-dates*) of Ibn Zabr al-Raba'i (d. 379/989). On the same topic, he read with Abu Muhammad Hibat Allah b. Ahmad Ibn al-Akfani (d. 524/1129) another book by al-Khatib al-Baghdadi entitled *Talkhis al-Mutashabah* (*The Concise Treatise on Distinguishing Names and Name-spelling of Hadith Scholars*), and a book on the questionable transmitters of Hadith entitled *Kitab al-Du'afa'* (*On the Weak Transmitters of Hadiths*) by Abu Zur'a al-Razi (d. 264/878) as preserved by Sa'id b. 'Amr al-Bardha'i (d. 292/905). Ibn al-Akfani also taught him *Kitab al-Ta'rikh* (*On History*) and *Kitab al-Tabaqat* (*On Generations*), both by Abu Zur'a al-Dimashqi (d. 282/895); *Kitab Ta'rikh Darayya* (*History of Darayya*) by Ibn Muhanna al-Khawlani (d. c. 370/980); and gave him a certificate to transmit the *Ta'rikh Baghdad*.

In Damascus too, Ibn 'Asakir met Abu Tahir Isma'il b. Nasr al-Tusi (d. 519/1125) who granted him a certificate to transmit

Kitab Fada'il bayt al-maqdis wa-l-khalil wa-fada'il al-sham (*The Merits of Jerusalem, Hebron, and Syria*) of Abu al-Ma'ali Ibn al-Murajja al-Maqdisi (d. after 438/1047). He also met Abu al-Qasim Nasr b. Ahmad al-Susi (d. 548/1153) who gave him a certificate to transmit *Kitab Fada'il al-bayt al-muqaddas* (*The Merits of Jerusalem*) of Abu Bakr al-Wasiti (d. after 410/1019), and Abu al-Faraj Ghayth b. 'Ali al-Suri (d. 509/1115) who taught him *Kitab al-Kharaj* (*On Taxation*) of Qudama b. Ja'far (d. 337/948) in addition to two other books, one entitled *Ta'rikh Sur* (*History of Tyre*) and the other *Kitab fih akhbar al-Ka'ba wa-fada'iluha wa-asma' al-mudun wa-l-buldan wa-akhbaruha* (*On the History of the Ka'ba and Its Merits, and the Names and History of Cities and Places*). He also learned *Kitab Adab al-katib* (*On the Etiquette of Writers*) of Ibn Qutayba (d. 276/889) with Abu al-Hasan 'Ali b. al-Hasan al-'Attar (d. 522/1128), as well as *Mushkil al-Qur'an* (*The Unclear in the Qur'an*) of al-Khatib al-Baghdadi and parts of *Ta'rikh Baghdad*.

The topic of the conquests of Syria (*Futuh al-Sham*) seems to have been of great interest to Ibn 'Asakir. He received a certificate to transmit *Kitab Futuh al-Sham* (*On the Conquests of Syria*) of al-Qudami (d. c. 205/820) from Subay' b. al-Musallam and Abu al-Qasim al-Nasib. He also had a copy of it written by 'Abd al-Wahid and 'Abd al-'Aziz, sons of Muhammad b. 'Abdawayh al-Shirazi (both fl. late-fourth to early fifth century and lived in Damascus). In addition, he read *Kitab al-Maghazi* (*History of the Prophet's Raids*) of Muhammad b. 'A'idh (d. c. 233/847) with Ibn al-Akfani and Abu al-Hasan al-Sulami.

Moreover, Hibat Allah arranged for Ibn 'Asakir to have certificates from a few scholars in Baghdad and other cities in the Muslim East. For instance, Abu 'Ali al-Hasan b. Ahmad al-Haddad (d. 515/1121) of Isfahan gave him a certificate to transmit the *Mu'jam al-kabir* (*Great Compendium of Hadiths*) of al-Tabarani (d. 360/971) and several works by Abu Nu'aym al-Isfahani (d. 529/1038), including *Kitab al-Qadar* (*On Predestination*) and *Kitab Ma'rifat al-sahaba* (*On Identifying the Companions*). Abu Talib al-Husayn b. Muhammad al-Zaynabi (d. 512/118) of Baghdad also sent him a certificate to transmit *Kitab Ta'rikh al-himsiyyin* (*History and Biographies of the Residents of Hims*) of Ahmad b. Muhammad al-Baghdadi (d. c. 305/917).

These kinds of details might seem tedious for those unfamiliar with medieval Islamic history and education. (Readers should feel free to skip the following sections on Ibn 'Asakir's two educational journeys if they wish.) Nevertheless, the importance of this seemingly tedious information is that it allows us to really grasp the exceptional nature of his quest, especially given the time and effort these journeys and Ibn 'Asakir's intensive study demanded. This approach to learning resulted in the best education an aspiring scholar of Hadith could receive, yet only a few were able to undertake such an ambitious pursuit. Moreover, the books Ibn 'Asakir studied during his two trips and the scholars with whom he studied them gave him access to the foundational sources of the Sunni Hadith cannon and its sciences in ways that had not been accomplished previously by any Damascene scholar.

In short, Ibn 'Asakir returned to Damascus equipped with an impressive resume of exceptional teachers he had studied under and a treasure trove of essential Hadith sources that truly impressed the people of the city. Now, they had their very own master of Hadith they could depend on; no longer would they be dependent on scholars from elsewhere, however notable, who had taken up a brief residence in Damascus as part of their pilgrimage or Sufi retreat. Such an education not only allowed Ibn 'Asakir to launch a successful career and produce the rich scholarship that has had an enduring impact on Sunni thought, it afforded him a level of prestige well above most of his local peers. It was this education that also awed later generations, as they realized the character of its extraordinary quality. In today's world, Ibn 'Asakir might be compared to someone who spent more than ten years travelling to the best universities around the globe, studying the most important books of a given discipline with the most distinguished professors, before launching a scholarly career. Ibn 'Asakir's educational journey was a colossal undertaking; only a careful analysis of its intricate details can truly reveal its exceptionality.

It is also important to bear in mind the time and effort required to study each individual book with a professor, the need to meet for several days, or weeks in some cases, to carefully review it in its entirety in order to achieve mastery of it. The culture and methods of education in the Muslim world at the time were very specific. Teaching often occurred at the main mosque of the town or in the house of the teacher. The gradual establishment of colleges (*madrasas*) starting in the fifth/eleventh century introduced new centers of education better equipped for practical and logistical needs, but there were not enough of them to meet the demand until well after Ibn 'Asakir's time.

Students had to travel from town to town, seeking out each professor individually to study with him or her. They might arrive at a town only to find that a certain professor was not there; depending on the importance of that professor, they might decide to stay in the area until the professor returned, try to catch him/her wherever the professor was visiting, or simply give up and seek to study with someone else. Sometimes, students arrived at a destination only to hear that the professor they had travelled so far to meet and study with had just passed away. Certainly, when students left their hometowns to embark on their educational journeys, they already had an idea of where they wanted to go and with whom they wanted to study. But the uncertainties of life, coupled with the days, weeks, even months it took for news to travel from one location to another, mandated that they improvise. In addition, as they travelled, students gathered information about other eminent professors and scholars they might want to study with, and altered their itinerary accordingly. This, too, introduced an element of uncertainty regarding the time it took to accomplish one's desired goals. Coming from a well-to-do family and having an already established reputation as a budding young scholar, Ibn 'Asakir's travels do not appear to have been constrained by any external limitations (family demands, financial burdens, health issues, and so on). Nor does it appear that he placed any restrictions on himself in his far-flung pursuit of knowledge.

First Trip

In 520/1126, Ibn 'Asakir embarked on his first extensive educational journey, which lasted for five years. He resided mainly in Baghdad, where he studied at the Nizamiyya College and became the student of several notable Hanbali scholars, learning Sunni and Hanbali law with Abu al-Husayn Muhammad b. Muhammad Ibn Abu Ya'la al-Farra' (d. 526/1131) and Hadith – including the *Musnad* (*Prophetic Traditions Listed According to the Companions Who Transmitted Them*) of Ahmad Ibn Hanbal (d. 241/855) – with Abu al-Qasim Hibat Allah b. Muhammad Ibn al-Husayn (d. 525/1131) and Abu al-Fadl Muhammad b. Nasir al-Hafiz (d. 551/1156). The latter also taught him the *Ta'rikh al-kabir* (*Major Compendium of Hadith Scholars*) of al-Bukhari (d. 256/870), and the *Kitab Ishtiqaq asma' al-buldan* (*On the Origins of Place Names*) of Abu al-Husayn Ahmad b. Faris al-Lughawi (d. 395/1004). Additionally, Ibn 'Asakir had received a written certificate to transmit al-Bukhari's *Ta'rikh* from Abu al-Ghana'im Muhammad b. 'Ali Ibn al-Nursi al-Kufi (510/1116) without having met him in person. It is likely that Hibat Allah had arranged this certificate for his sibling while on his own travels for his education.

While in Baghdad, Ibn 'Asakir also studied Hadith with Abu Ghalib Ahmad b. al-Hasan Ibn al-Banna' (d. 527/1133) who gave him a certificate to transmit the *Kitab al-Jihad* (*Book of Jihad*) of Ibn al-Mubarak (d. 181/797) and the *Tabaqat* of Ibn Sa'd. There, too, he met Abu Sa'd Isma'il b. Abu Salih al-Naysaburi (d. 532/1138) and studied Islamic law with him, especially the matters of disagreement in Sunni jurisprudence, and Abu al-Qasim Isma'il b. Ahmad Ibn al-Samarqandi (d. 536/1142) who gave him a certificate to transmit the *Kitab Futuh al-Sham* (*On the Conquests of Syria*) of Ishaq b. Bishr al-Bukhari (d. 206/821), *Kitab Tabaqat al-shu'ara' al-jahiliyyin* (*Dictionary of Pre-Islamic Poets*) of Muhammad b. Sallam al-Jumahi (d. c. 232/846), *Kitab Ta'rikh Jurjan* (*History of Jurjan*) of al-Jurjani (d. 427/1036), and *Kitab Tabaqat al-fuqaha'* (*Dictionary of Jurists*) of Abu Ishaq al-Shirazi (d. 476/1083).

Ibn 'Asakir also received a certificate from Abu al-Qasim Sadaqa b. Muhammad al-Mahlaban (d. 551/1156) to transmit the *Kitab Ta'rikh al-Andalus* (*History of Islamic Spain and Biographies of Muslims There*) – also known as *Juzwat al-muqtabas fi dhikr wulat al-andalus* – of al-Humaydi (d. 488/1095), a certificate to transmit *Kitab Ta'rikh al-Riqqa* (*History of Riqqa*) of al-Harrani (d. after 334/945) from Abu Bakr Muhammad b. al-Husayn al-Mazrafi (d. 527/1132), and another certificate to transmit all the works of Abu Ja'far Ahmad Ibn Mihriz al-Shatibi (d.

after 516/1123), including the one on the seven recitations of the Qur'an entitled *al-Muqni' fi al-qira'at al-sab'a* (*The Persuasive Book on the Seven Readings*).

Ibn 'Asakir benefitted from his stay in Baghdad to travel to other towns in Iraq, and even perform his first pilgrimage to Mecca in 521/1127, where he studied with local scholars. On his way there, he stopped in Kufa in Dhu al-Qa'da 521/November 1127, and on his way back he visited Medina in Muharram 522/January 1128 to study there as well. He departed for Damascus in early 525/early 1131, stopping in al-Anbar and al-Rahaba.

Second Trip

Following a few years in Damascus, during which time his first child al-Qasim was born in 527/1133, Ibn 'Asakir embarked on his second educational journey in Muharram 529/October 1134. It lasted four years and took him to the eastern Muslim world, visiting and studying in such cities as Tabriz and Zanjan in Jumada I 529/February 1135, and Nishapur in Sha'ban 529/June 1136. Shortly after his arrival in Nishapur, he met Abu Sa'd 'Abd al-Karim b. Muhammad al-Sam'ani (d. 562/1166), who became a famous scholar of Hadith and wrote *Kitab al-Ansab* (*Book of Lineages*) and also compiled a continuation of al-Khatib al-Baghdadi's *Ta'rikh*. The two spent some time together studying there and became lifelong companions; it is probably this friendship that cemented the strong Ash'ari and anti-Hanbali stance in both scholars (which will be discussed in Chapter 3).

In Nishapur, Ibn 'Asakir studied with Abu al-Muzaffar 'Abd al-Mun'im b. 'Abd al-Karim (d. 532/1138), the son of the celebrated mystic and Hadith scholar Abu al-Qasim al-Qushayri (d. 465/1073), and with al-Qushayri's granddaughter Durdana bt. Isma'il (d. 530/1135). He also met Abu al-Qasim Zahir b. Tahir al-Shahhami (d. 533/1138) who taught him the *Sunan* (*Prophetic Traditions*) of al-Bayhaqi (d. 458/1066). In Nishapur, he sought out one scholar in particular, Abu 'Abd Allah Muhammad b. al-Fadl al-Furawi (d. 530/1136), who taught Ibn 'Asakir *Dala'il al-nubuwwa* (*Proofs of Muhammad's Prophethood*) of al-Bayhaqi and, more importantly, all the major books of the Hadith canon: *Sahih* (*Authentic Hadiths*) of al-Bukhari, *Sahih* of Muslim (d. 261/875), *Sunan* (*Prophetic Traditions*) of Abu Dawud (d. 275/889), *Jami' al-kabir* (*Great Compendium of Hadiths*) of al-Tirmidhi (d. 279/892), and *Sunan al-kubra* (*Great Compendium of Prophetic Traditions*) of al-Nasa'i (d. 303/915). During this period, Ibn 'Asakir developed a reputation as an ambitious seeker of religious scholarship, which in some cases irritated his teachers. We are told, for instance, that after three days studying with al-Furawi, the latter became bored and decided to turn down Ibn 'Asakir the next day. That morning, however, a person showed up at his door claiming to have seen the Prophet Muhammad in a dream telling him to convey a message to al-Furawi to be patient with the "young dark-skinned Syrian" and teach him Hadith.

After Nishapur, Ibn 'Asakir moved to Herat, arriving there in Sha'ban 530/May 1136 and then to Merv in Rabi' I 531/December 1136. He also visited many towns in Khurasan (around Nishapur, Herat and Merv, which today is located between northeastern Iran and northwestern Afghanistan), staying there until Sha'ban 531/April 1137. After that, he turned westwards, stopping on his way at Bistam in Muharram 532/September 1137 and al-Rayy in Muharram 532/October 1137, and arriving at his other main destination, Isfahan, in Safar 532/late October 1137. There he met, among others, Abu al-Fath Yusuf b. 'Abd al-Wahid al-Baqillani (d. 540/1145) and received from him several certificates, including one to transmit *Kitab Ma'rifat al-sahaba* (*On Identifying the Companions*) of Ibn Manda (d. 395/1005). He also met Abu 'Abd Allah al-Husayn b. 'Abd al-Malik al-Adib (d. 532/1138) shortly before his death, and studied with him the *Musnad* (*Prophetic Traditions Listed According to the Companions who Transmitted Them*) of Abu Ya'la al-Mawsili (d. 307/919).

Ibn 'Asakir then moved northwest to Mushkan near Hamadhan (today in western Iran), arriving in Dhu al-Hijja 532/August 1138. There he met the orator (*khatib*) of the Friday mosque Abu al-Hasan 'Ali b. Muhammad al-Rawdhrawari (d. 550/1155) who taught him the *Ta'rikh al-saghir* (*Minor Compendium on Hadith Scholars*) of al-Bukhari; he then visited Hamadhan. On his way back to Damascus, he stopped for a few weeks in Baghdad in 533/1138 where he saw his companion al-Sam'ani. He also met Muhammad b. al-Fadl al-Isfarayini (d. 538/ 1144) and attended a few classes with him on Ash'ari theology. He was back in his hometown before the end of the year 533/early summer 1139.

There are other books that Ibn 'Asakir knew and frequently quoted in his Ta'rikh, but he did not say who taught him these books, and given he did not provide chains of transmission for them it seems unlikely that he had certificates to transmit them. These books include Kitab al-Aghani (Book of Songs) of Abu al-Faraj al-Isfahani (d. 356/967), Kitab Umara' Dimashq (On the Rulers of Damascus) attributed to Ishaq b. Qubaysa al-Khuza'i (d. c. 105/724), Kitab Ishtiqaq asma' al-qaba'il (On the Origins of the Names of Tribes) of Ibn Durayd al-Basri (d. 321/933), Kitab al-Alqab (On Nicknames) of Abu Bakr al-Shirazi (d. 388/998), and many others.

As noted earlier, this detailed sketch of Ibn 'Asakir's two educational trips and list of which works he studied and with whom in the different cities he visited appear to be rather dry reading. But it is precisely this information that is essential for understanding the extraordinary effort Ibn 'Asakir exerted to attain the astounding mastery of the sciences of Hadith that caused his fellow Damascenes to revere him the way they did. A close examination of his curriculum vitae indicates that during his first trip he pursued an array of subjects, but that during the second trip he focused almost exclusively on Hadith and a few related fields. Apparently, he had already decided to narrow his intellectual pursuits to Hadith prior to his departure from Damascus in 529/1134.

Return to Damascus

As a result of these travels, Ibn 'Asakir returned to his hometown with an impressive knowledge of Hadith and an astonishing resume of male teachers, totaling, according to his Mu'jam al-shuyukh (Catalogue of Teachers) (see Chapter 3), around 1,700. He also studied with more than eighty women teachers; he wrote a similar catalogue for them but, unfortunately, it seems to be lost. This educational pedigree positioned Ibn 'Asakir for prominence among his peers and earned him two honorifics: *al-Hafiz* (the great memorizer of Hadith) and *Nasir al-Sunna* (advocate of the Sunna of the Prophet Muhammad).

There was another much more profound impact of Ibn 'Asakir's educational journey. It is said that he was the first scholar to bring copies of books that were not known in Damascus and to disseminate them in the city, such as the *Musnad* of Ibn Hanbal and the *Musnad* of Abu Ya'la al-Mawsili (this aspect will be picked up later in Chapters 3 and 6).

An interesting marginal note about Ibn 'Asakir's second educational journey is that, despite the many certificates that he received to transmit books, especially in Nishapur, he did not bring his own copies back with him to Damascus. He left them behind with two of his colleagues, hoping that one of them at least would journey westwards and bring them with him. However, neither of them did. He agonized that the valuable knowledge he had learned in the east was lost, and was on the verge of leaving for a third trip when an old companion, Abu al-Hasan 'Ali b. Sulayman al-Muradi (d. 544/1150), arrived in Damascus, shortly after 540/1145. He brought with him two camel loads of his own books, most of which he had studied together with Ibn 'Asakir in Khurasan. Ibn 'Asakir spent several weeks copying them, which not only allowed him to enrich his own writings, but more crucially he could now teach them in Damascus and give his students certificates to transmit them.

TEACHING AND CHARACTER

Upon his return to his hometown in the early summer of 533/1139, the local scholarly community asked Ibn 'Asakir to start teaching Hadith in the Umayyad Mosque. His maternal grandfather, Abu al-Mufaddal Yahya, had a hand in arranging this, for it is said that when he saw Ibn 'Asakir upon his return from the second journey, he told him "sit in the mosque so that we can sit around you and learn from what you have learned." Ibn 'Asakir obliged. This is how he got his first teaching opportunity in the Umayyad Mosque, joining a distinguished, albeit restricted list of elite scholars there.

Ibn 'Asakir's main teaching occurred in the Umayyad Mosque. He gave there a weekly seminar (*majlis**), on different topics, all involving Hadith. They total more than 408 seminars, and some of them are still extant. For instance, he gave his 52nd seminar entitled *Fi dhamm al-malahi* (*On Censuring Amusement*) on 17 Shawwal 538/23 April 1144, which engaged hadiths that scorn and ridicule those who pursue amusement and social trivialities. He gave his 53rd seminar on 25 Shawwal 538/1 May 1144 entitled *Fi dhamm qurana' al-su'* (*On Censuring Bad Acquaintances*), which featured several hadiths on companionship and the need to remain vigilant about whom to befriend.

These seminars went on for several years, and Ibn 'Asakir repeated them a few times. For example, he retaught seminar no. 238 entitled *Fi fadl Sa'd b. Abi Waqqas* (*On the Virtues of Sa'd b. Abu Waqqas*), who was one of the most celebrated Companions of Muhammad, on 4 Sha'ban 544/7 December 1149 in the Umayyad Mosque, and two months before that – on 8 Jumada II 543/24 October 1148 – he retaught seminar no. 280 entitled *Fi fadl 'Abd Allah Ibn Mas'ud* (*On the Virtues of 'Abd Allah Ibn Mas'ud*), another celebrated Companion known mostly for his own codex of the Qur'an.

Ibn 'Asakir repeated these seminars again in the period 550/1155–551/1156, which is attested by the extant manuscripts that record them. For example, he retaught seminar no. 14 entitled *Fi dhamm man la ya'mal bi-'ilmih* (*On Censuring Those Who Do Not Use Their Knowledge*) on 11 Muharram 550/17 March 1155, seminar no. 32 entitled *Fi al-tawba* (*On Repentance*) in Safar 550/April 1155, and seminar no. 46 entitled *Fi fadl 'A'isha* (*On the Virtues of 'A'isha*), the celebrated wife of the Prophet Muhammad, on 19 Jumada I 550/21 July 1155. We do not know when he taught them for the first time, but it must have been either in 536/1142 or 537/1143.

We do not know when exactly he started holding his classes at the Umayyad Mosque under the Eagle's Dome (*Qubbat al-Nisr*), which was the highest honor a scholar could attain in Damascus, and which remained the case up to the early twentieth century. It both highlights his scholarly distinction and, more importantly, the great esteem of his colleagues who would bestow on him such a privilege.

Later on, in the early 560s/mid-1160s, and due to the close relationship he developed with Sultan Nur al-Din (as we will see in Chapter 3), Ibn 'Asakir also taught at Nur al-Din's College of Hadith (known as *Dar al-Hadith al-Nuriyya* or *Dar al-Sunna*). This College, we are told, was built by Nur al-Din specifically for Ibn 'Asakir, as a recognition of his scholarly distinction and reward for his involvement in the jihad propaganda that the Sultan was sponsoring (for more on the College of Hadith and Ibn 'Asakir's teaching, see Chapter 3).

With respect to his character, Ibn 'Asakir was both a person that many admired profoundly, yet one who seems to have been inclined to remind his contemporaries of his own importance. Indeed, medieval literature contains many anecdotes about his haughtiness. Al-Dhahabi, for instance, expressed a telling remark that Ibn 'Asakir "never met someone like himself." Others, like 'Imad al-Din al-Isfahani (d. 597/1201), even contrasted Ibn 'Asakir's arrogant demeanor to the pleasant and charming personality of his brother Hibat Allah.

Ibn 'Asakir's sense of self-importance reveals not only what he thought of his own scholarly merit, but more importantly the crucial role he was destined to play in the renewal of Sunnism in Damascus, Syria and beyond. The words of his son al-Qasim draw our attention to these two aspects:

> I used to hear my father say that, while his mother was pregnant with
> him, his father had a vision in a dream informing him that he would
> beget a son whom God would use to revivify Sunnism.
>
> (Yaqut al-Hamawi, *Mu'jam al-udaba'* 4: 1702)

In another report, also attributed to al-Qasim, Ibn 'Asakir confided to him that at the beginning of the pregnancy, his mother heard a voice in her dream telling her:

> You will beget a child who will become very important. When you
> deliver him, bring him on the fortieth day of his birth to the Grotto –
> meaning the Grotto of Blood in the Mount Qasyun – and give alms, for
> then God will bless him and bless the Muslims by him.
>
> (Al-Subki, *Tabaqat al-shafi'iyya* 4: 139)

The Grotto of Blood was a cave in Mount Qasyun (to the northwest of the city) believed by the locals to be the location where Cain murdered his brother Abel (Genesis 4.1–12). Hence, the "blood" is that of the righteous Abel. It was therefore one of the sacred spots around Damascus where people sought (even today) divine blessing.

Another anecdote was recounted by al-Qasim from his father:

> One day I was studying with Abu al-Fath al-Mukhtar b. 'Abd al-Hamid, and he turned to the people who were present and said: "When Abu 'Ali Ibn al-Wazir came to study with us, we said that we have seen none like him, then came Abu Sa'd al-Sam'ani and we said that we have seen none like him. Now this one comes, and truly, we have seen none like him."
>
> (Ibn Kathir, *Tabaqat al-fuqaha' al-shafi'iyyin* 694–695)

Abu al-Fath al-Mukhtar b. 'Abd al-Hamid al-Fushanji (d. 536/1142) was a notable scholar of Hadith who taught Ibn 'Asakir in Herat during the latter's second educational trip. It was indeed common for teachers to share their assessments of their students. Yet, what is interesting for our consideration here is that Ibn 'Asakir himself collected these assessments and disseminated them, which demonstrates his awareness of his own scholarly worthiness, but also his eagerness that others know about it as well.

Al-Qasim also reported that his father once told him the names of the most impressive memorizers of Hadith he had met in every city or region. Al-Qasim said to him: "I swear you are better than all of them." Ibn 'Asakir did not say a word in response to that. This is corroborated in a similar anecdote by one of Ibn 'Asakir's closest students, Abu al-Mawahib al-Hasan b. Hibat Allah Ibn Sasra (d. 586/1190), who related that he used to ask Ibn 'Asakir about the great memorizers of Hadith he had met, and Ibn 'Asakir would name them. Ibn Sasra remarked: "According to what you said, O master, you have met none like yourself!" Ibn 'Asakir objected: "Do not say that, for almighty God says: 'Do not acclaim your own virtues' (Qur'an 53.32)." Ibn Sasra retorted: "But God also said, 'And your Lord's blessing proclaim!' (Qur'an 93.11)." Ibn 'Asakir then responded: "Yes, if someone else said that he saw none like me, he would be correct." (Al-Subki, *Tabaqat al-shafi'iyya* 4: 142)

Such evidence exhibits how highly Ibn 'Asakir considered himself vis-à-vis his peers, especially in Damascus. His self-esteem, bordering on haughtiness, is also displayed in some of his works. For example, in his treatise on jihad, *al-Arba'un hadith fi al-hathth 'ala al-jihad* (which will be discussed in Chapter 3), he quoted forty hadiths praising warfare and fighters. In all but one case, he completely ignored his Damascene teachers who we know taught him hadiths on jihad. That he chose to ignore their transmission of the same hadiths he quoted from other teachers he met in Baghdad, Isfahan, Nishapur, and elsewhere is indicative of his sense of self-importance, and his eagerness to display his mastery of Hadith in Damascus and make the point that he did not owe this mastery to the teachers in his hometown.

Ibn 'Asakir was also fond of poetry. Both his *Ta'rikh* as well as his *Mu'jam al-shuyukh* include many poems he heard from his teachers, and at the end of each of his books, even his weekly seminars, he concluded with a relevant poem. He also composed a lot of poetry himself. But many did not think highly of its quality. Yaqut al-Hamawi (d. 626/1229), who quoted a few lines in Ibn 'Asakir's biography in *Mu'jam al-udaba'* (*Catalogue of Authors*), said the following: "He used to compose poetry, which was not that good." Another Damascene scholar described Ibn 'Asakir's poetic prowess in the following manner: "This poetry is by one who has lost his demon," the point here stemming from the commonplace belief that every poet has a demon that inspires him/her.

Ibn 'Asakir's haughty attitude was not, however, the reason for his animosity towards the local Hanbalis. This is rather intriguing, given the fact that during his first educational trip to Baghdad, he was close to some of the leading Hanbali scholars of the time. The animosity with the local Hanbalis stemmed from a combination of local politics and theological differences (as we will see in Chapter 3). It somehow undermined his ability to rise above local politics and appeal to all Sunni scholars in Damascus. The Hanbalis remained aloof towards him for several generations, and it seems that it was Ibn Taymiyya (d. 728/1128) who succeeded in partially rehabilitating Ibn 'Asakir's image among the Hanbalis in the city.

WRITINGS

Ibn 'Asakir wrote many works; probably more than 100 (if one counts the books and the published seminars). They range from multi-volume works to short treatises (for a list of the extant books by Ibn 'Asakir, see the Bibliography at the end). The two most important books are his massive biographical encyclopedia *Ta'rikh Dimashq* (*History of Damascus*), which will be extensively discussed in Chapter 4, and *Tabyin kadhib al-muftari* (*Exposing the Slanderer's Mendacity*), which will be examined in Chapter 3.

Al-Dhahabi gave a list of fifty-two works Ibn 'Asakir supposedly authored, but it is not accurate and it does not include the seminars. Ibn 'Asakir's son al-Qasim compiled two lists of books. One list comprised the titles he was sure his father wrote. The other list contained works he never saw but which he believed his father had started or intended to write. Al-Dhahabi took both lists and collated them. Thus, it is important to limit our discussion to the actual works that Ibn 'Asakir finished, and not those he planned to write or that others thought he wrote.

Most of Ibn 'Asakir's works focus on Hadith, and even those that are not strictly speaking Hadith books contain a great many prophetic traditions, showing that for him Hadith was the cornerstone of religious knowledge and history. For instance, *Ta'rikh Dimashq* contains around 15,000 prophetic hadiths, which are dispersed throughout the work. They feature in the individual biographies of people, either because they transmitted a hadith or they were the subject of one. Also, Ibn 'Asakir's books and treatises on the religious merits of many locales and shrines in and around Damascus are mostly collections of prophetic hadiths and anecdotes about them, as well as biblical legends linked to events that allegedly occurred there, and stories about Companions and Successors* who lived there. In this respect, it is noteworthy that Ibn 'Asakir considered the act of transmitting prophetic Hadith to be an important religious virtue, which transferred religious merits to the places where the transmission occurred.

DEATH

Ibn 'Asakir died in Damascus on Sunday evening, 11 Rajab 571/25
January 1176. His funeral was attended by a very large crowd. Leading
the burial prayer were Qutb al-Din al-Naysaburi (d. 578/1183),
the chief-judge of Damascus and the leader of the Shafi'is, as well as
Sultan Saladin. It was held in the open field of Midan al-Hasa (today
known as al-Midan) on the southern side of the city. He was interred
in the nearby cemetery of Bab al-Saghir (the Small Gate) next to his
deceased family members and adjacent to the grave of Umayyad Caliph
Mu'awiya (r. 40/661–60/680), who was his maternal ancestor. It
is said that though the winter was dry that year, when Ibn 'Asakir's
coffin was lifted to be carried to the tomb, it poured as if heaven was
weeping on him.

3

SCHOLARSHIP AND ACTIVISM

Ibn 'Asakir was an ardent advocate of Sunnism. His career and writings reveal that he understood Islam and its teachings as revolving around the Sunna of the Prophet Muhammad. It, and it alone, plays the exclusive role of unlocking the message of the Qur'an and the lessons of history, defines for Muslims matters of belief and conduct, and charts the way forward. Moreover, that he spent his life pursuing hadiths and disseminating them attests to his awareness of his own role in the revivification of Sunni Islam as revolving around the Sunna of Muhammad, especially in his hometown Damascus, and also in assisting his fellow Muslims to attain salvation by making Hadith accessible to them.

The revivification of Sunnism was a major desire among the Syrian elites, given the political and religious realities in Syria in the fifth/eleventh century and the fact that the Sunnis there were relatively weak (as discussed in Chapter 1). This was the world into which Ibn 'Asakir was born and started his educational journey. The eastern part of the Muslim world was both the political and intellectual center of Sunnism. By the time of his death, the situation had shifted in favor of Syria, and there is every reason to believe that Ibn 'Asakir was among those who made this possible. His scholarship and teaching were instrumental in creating a Sunni intellectual renaissance in Damascus, but one should not ignore the fact that he was also keen to deploy his scholarly and pedagogical talents in the service of his political patron, Nur al-Din, and the political and religious agendas of the Sultan.

Indeed, Ibn 'Asakir helped shape the religious agenda of Sultan Nur al-Din, and some of his works were instrumental in propagating it. Moreover, his uncompromising passion for Sunnism informed his reaction to political events and religious life in Syria. One of his concerns, which many fellow Sunnis at the time also shared, was the disunity among Muslims and the threat posed to Islam by the Shi'is and Crusaders. In their collective consciousness, this concern demanded the rise of a powerful Sunni sultan to fight for and achieve this unity and bring about the revival of Sunni Islam, especially in Syria and Egypt.

Ibn 'Asakir's activism must also be assessed not only on the basis of his books, but equally by taking into account the more than 408 seminars he gave on different topics, and which he repeated on several occasions throughout the course of his career. Some of these seminars have actually survived. If they convey anything about him and his beliefs, it is that Hadith has an answer to every single issue in life, be it theological, social, or personal. From denying anthropomorphism, to lauding jihad, to mourning a friend, from seeking repentance and God's mercy, to praising the fast of Ramadan and the memorization of the Qur'an, to avoiding bad companions and amusements; all of these issues are explained in the words of the Prophet Muhammad, as if Ibn 'Asakir were saying that apart from the Sunna, one needs nothing else.

Moreover, some of these seminars focused on major individuals in Islamic history, such as Caliphs Abu Bakr (r. 11/632–13/634), 'Umar (r. 13/634–23/644), 'Uthman (r. 23/644–35/656), and 'Ali (r. 36/656–40/661), Muhammad's widow 'A'isha (d. 58/678), and Companions Sa'd b. Abu Waqqas (d. c. 55/675) and 'Abd Allah Ibn Mas'ud (d. 32/653). These topics carried a subtle subtext as Sunnism was asserting itself as the main religious force in Damascus. Therefore, Ibn 'Asakir helped define not just any form of Sunnism but rather a specific kind of Sunnism along with its ideological contours and personalities (for more on this, see Chapter 4). Thus, his legacy in Sunni Islam as the revivifier of Sunnism.

POLITICAL UNITY AND REVIVIFICATION OF SUNNISM

The issues of political unity and revivification of Sunnism preoccupied Ibn 'Asakir and shaped his ideological formation, career, and activism.

This needs to be seen in light of three interconnected spheres: 1. anti-Shi'ism and the need for the political unity of Sunnis especially in Syria and Egypt, 2. the defense of Ash'arism against other Sunni rivals, and 3. the liberation of Jerusalem and jihad against Islam's external enemies.

As an ardent Sunni, Ibn 'Asakir considered Shi'ism to be a heresy. He addressed it on several occasions and devoted one of his seminars to it — On Denouncing the Heretical Sect (Fi dhamm al-Rafida), which is lost. The language that we find in his existing works allows us to form a good picture of his anti-Shi'i stance. For instance, in the biography of Nur al-Din in the Ta'rikh Dimashq, Ibn 'Asakir pointed out that the Sultan's most important accomplishments were the political unity of Syria and Egypt and the triumph of Sunnism, which allowed for the enactment of essential religious reforms in order to boost Sunnism and undermine Shi'i heresies. For example, he wrote the following about Nur al-Din's religious reforms in Aleppo:

> He restored Sunnism in Aleppo and re-established true religion. He corrected the heresy that they used to follow in the call for prayer, crushed the heretical Shi'is who were in the city, and promulgated the four Sunni branches of jurisprudence. He saved the people there from the obligation to supply provisions and barred them from involvement in internal wars. He built schools and set endowments, and spread justice and fairness throughout the city.
>
> (Ibn 'Asakir, Ta'rikh 57: 120)

Similarly, Ibn 'Asakir celebrated Nur al-Din's capture of Egypt, which he hailed as putting an end to Fatimid rule there. He said:

> Finally, the Sunnis were triumphant in Egypt and the sermons were read in the name of the Abbasid Caliph after almost complete despair. God had relieved the Egyptians from infighting and ended their suffering. Therefore, God is deserving of thanks for his graces and for allowing the conquest to succeed.
>
> (Ibn 'Asakir, Ta'rikh 57: 123)

It is beside the point that it actually took a few months before the sermons in Cairo and Egypt were read in the name of the Abbasid* Caliph. It is also the case that Asad al-Din Shirkuh (d. 564/1169) who led Nur al-Din's army into Egypt became the vizier of the Fatimid

Caliph al-'Adid li-Din Allah (r. 555/1160–566/1171), and Fatimid
rule over Egypt only ended in 566/1171 when al-'Adid died and
Saladin (who succeeded his uncle Shirkuh as vizier) did not allow a
Fatimid successor to be sworn in. Moreover, Saladin had his own
designs to keep Egypt for himself, with only nominal submission to
his boss Nur al-Din.

Historical accuracy notwithstanding, the words of Ibn 'Asakir
reveal how he – and no doubt, many other Sunni scholars at the time
who shared his persuasion – perceived the events and their ramifi-
cations, and hoped that their aspirations for unity would become a
reality. Thus, Nur al-Din's career, according to Ibn 'Asakir, was
crowned with the achievement of the revivification of Sunnism, both
as a political and religious power in Syria and Egypt following a long,
dark epoch of Shi'i domination. Furthermore, given the fact that Ibn
'Asakir considered himself one of the architects of the Sunni revival,
these words demonstrate that he considered Shi'is and Shi'ism as
major impediments. Consequently, ending their power and their heresies added another jewel to Nur al-Din's crown.

Moreover, the revivification of Sunnism and achieving political
unity would allow the Muslims to confront successfully their external
enemies. Indeed, we see how Ibn 'Asakir tied together the two aspects
in the following poem. It was preserved by 'Imad al-Din al-Isfahani,
who said that Ibn 'Asakir dictated it to him on 22 Jumada I 564/21
February 1169 to convey to Nur al-Din as a congratulatory message
for "capturing" Egypt:

> Because you exempted the Damascenes from the levy of wood, / you
> were compensated with Egypt and its plentiful goods.
>
> Should you endeavor to conquer Jerusalem, / your reward shall be
> great, a recompense beyond calculation.
>
> For the reward of God is already set; / indeed, deeds that merit his
> reward are a better bet.
>
> As for renown among people, you have earned it; / it is worthier
> than the purest silver and gold.
>
> Yet, you shall receive no pardon should you forsake jihad, for / you
> now rule from Egypt to Aleppo.
>
> Even the Lord of Mosul complies / with your wishes, so hasten to
> issue the call to arms.

The most steadfast of people is he who toughens his resolve, / that he may attain the loftiest of ranks.

Good fortune and determination are bound together, / tenacity with steadfast intention; achievement with pursuit.

So, cleanse the Aqsa Sanctuary and its environs / from impurity, polytheism and the crucifixes.

May you earn in this world honorable acclaim / and on the Day of Resurrection a splendid welcome.

('Imad al-Din al-Isfahani, *Kharidat al-qasr* 1: 276–277)

In this poem, Ibn 'Asakir raised a few important issues that he saw as fundamental to the legitimacy of the Muslim ruler. First, the importance of seizing Egypt from the Fatimids and achieving the political unity with Syria – *you now rule from Egypt to Aleppo* – which was, as mentioned earlier, the earnest desire of many local Sunni religious activists at the time. Such an achievement, however, only placed, in Ibn 'Asakir's opinion, additional, more arduous responsibilities on the Sultan. Nur al-Din had no option but to turn all his attention and effort to the liberation of Jerusalem, for therein lay the greatest of rewards: *Should you endeavor to conquer Jerusalem, / your reward shall be great, a recompense beyond calculation.* It is only by pursuing this greatest of goals that Nur al-Din could attain, according to Ibn 'Asakir, the greatest of rewards: *On the Day of Resurrection a splendid welcome.*

There are clear indications that the liberation of Jerusalem was on the mind of Nur al-Din. For instance, he paid for the construction of a remarkable pulpit (*minbar*) that he intended to install in the mosque of the Aqsa Sanctuary upon its liberation. However, for a variety of reasons, he never launched a systematic campaign to liberate Jerusalem, but this was a distant objective. Moreover, as noted in Chapter 1, his dealings with the Franks featured a mixed policy of war and peace. Nur al-Din's death in 569/1174 passed this ambitious task to his Ayyubid successors. Nevertheless, the minute he captured Egypt, Ibn 'Asakir reminded him of the next objective: the liberation of Jerusalem and the cleansing of the Aqsa Sanctuary. It tells us what was pressing in the mind of Ibn 'Asakir more so than in Nur al-Din's.

Moreover, these words, expressed by Ibn 'Asakir as the events were unfolding, were not written as later reflections on the past.

This is of tremendous importance because they reveal what Ibn 'Asakir thought at the moment and how he reacted when he received the news of the religious reforms in Aleppo and the alleged conquest of Egypt.

There is an additional point to discuss: Ibn 'Asakir's animosity towards Shi'ism. In his *Ta'rikh*, he included (as will be examined in Chapter 4) biographies for several Shi'i imams and their descendants, which was part of his ambition to "rehabilitate" some major Islamic figures. It is important, therefore, to distinguish between Ibn 'Asakir's open hostility towards Shi'ism and his exoneration of certain important imams – especially the early ones, such as 'Ali, al-Hasan and al-Husayn – from any role in the "heresies" that their Shi'i followers promulgated about them, not to mention the Shi'is' responsibility in splitting Islam. Hence, the Sunni term of choice, *al-Rafida*, which means those who refused to acknowledge the legitimacy of Caliphal succession and splintered the Muslim community, and which Ibn 'Asakir generally used to refer to the Shi'is. Moreover, these Shi'i imams were not figures of a distant past. They were very relevant to Ibn 'Asakir's own society given two important factors. First, the fact that many local Sunnis were recent converts from Shi'ism and some of them traced their lineage back to these Shi'i imams and from them to the Prophet Muhammad; these families later came to be known as the *Ashraf* (nobles) of Damascus (there were other similar groups in other cities as well). Second, the fact that many descendants of the three imams mentioned above were interred in and around Damascus and their burial places were revered as quasi-sacred spots by Sunnis and Shi'is alike (and remain so today).

TRUSTEE OF HADITH

As mentioned earlier, the project of the revivification of Sunnism, for Ibn 'Asakir, centered around Hadith. If Islam is to be defined on the basis of the Sunna of the Prophet Muhammad, then Hadith scholarship is the central religious science. Here is what he says about the prophetic traditions and their importance:

Almighty God created his creation from mud ... and sent to them a
prophet from among them ... He [the Prophet] ordered his blessed
community to seek Hadith scholarship even unto China, so that when
they learn it they can distinguish between the unsound and sound
matters. He also promised salvation for whoever memorizes forty
hadiths relating to religion, intending with that to inform and instruct
his own community and seeking to guide them to attain the precious and
substantial and to shelter them from basing their religion on doubt and
conjecture... For doing that and due to his mercy, almighty God will
reward them by making them join the right flank, and in his abode of
magnificence, he will marry them to the heavenly dark-eyed virgins.

(Ibn 'Asakir, *al-Arba'un al-buldaniyya* 33–35)

These words by Ibn 'Asakir, which he often repeated in similar ways in
other books, reveal to us his understanding of the centrality of Hadith
in Islam. For him, the famous prophetic hadith – "seek knowledge
unto China" – was not meant to encourage the seeking of any knowledge. It precisely meant the seeking of hadiths, for Hadith alone allows
the believer to have certainty about matters instead of doubt and conjecture which come from other types of knowledge.

It is no surprise then that Ibn 'Asakir spent his entire career either
learning Hadith (by travelling to distant lands), teaching it, or writing
about it. Indeed, almost all of his books are actually Hadith compi-
lations or involve large numbers of hadiths, and they vary in length
from massive multi-volume works to small treatises, including several
books featuring forty hadiths, the coveted number that in his opinion would aid Muslims attaining the divine rewards: 1. joining the
Prophet Muhammad on the Day of Judgment by lining to his right
(which is the sign of those who are saved and will go to heaven, as
contrasted to those on his left side and who are doomed), and 2. wed-
ding the dark-eyed virgins (*hur al-'in*). For both images, Ibn 'Asakir
was obviously invoking Qur'an 56 (*Surat al-Qari'a* or the Calamity),
especially verses 8–40.

Moreover, Ibn 'Asakir's legacy in Sunnism (as we will see in
Chapter 6) was precisely his advocacy and dissemination of Hadith in
Damascus and Syria, at a time when such a level of proficiency was
lacking, unlike the case in Baghdad and other cities in the eastern parts
of the Muslim world (such as Isfahan and Nishapur).

It was Ibn 'Asakir's second trip that really cemented him as an authority on Hadith and probably reinforced his inclination to master all its related fields. His goal was not simply to learn hadiths, but rather to study and receive certificates for specific books, which were considered the foundational texts of Hadith, be they collections such as *Sahih* of al-Bukhari and *Sahih* of Muslim, or works that identify and assess the trustworthiness of Hadith transmitters. He was also eager to learn hadiths whose chains of transmission offer the shortest links to the Prophet Muhammad. It is in these domains that Ibn 'Asakir made his most important and lasting contribution: disseminating in Damascus the awareness and expertise about a specific Hadith canon and Hadith scholarship, which thanks in part to him became the canon for Sunnis everywhere. For instance, Baha' al-Din Ibn al-Jummayzi (d. 649/1252), who became one of the leading scholars of Hadith and Islamic law in Cairo, came to Damascus in 568/1173 specifically to study the *Sahih* of al-Bukhari with Ibn 'Asakir.

Ibn 'Asakir also taught countless classes, including more than 400 seminars at the Umayyad Mosque, some of which have been preserved by his students. They cover a large number of topics. In each seminar, Ibn 'Asakir narrated the hadiths that he had studied which related to the seminar's topic. They include several seminars on the first four Caliphs and a few major Companions. It is reported that once he gave seven lectures over several days on Caliph Abu Bakr (r. 11–13/632–634), and after that he gave a seminar entitled *Fi dhamm yahud al-Madina (On the Denunciation of the Jews of Medina)*. The next day one of his students came to him and said that the saw Abu Bakr in a dream and told the Caliph about Ibn 'Asakir's classes. Abu Bakr smiled and signaled back with four fingers. When Ibn 'Asakir heard this, he said to his student that, indeed, he had prepared four more lectures on Abu Bakr, which he went on to deliver in the following days. (This also shows how dreams – the one here and the ones discussed earlier – were instrumentalized in medieval society, even among the scholarly community.) The incident also inspired him to teach eleven classes on each of the three other Caliphs: 'Umar, 'Uthman, and 'Ali.

The College of Hadith

Sometime in the 560s/1160s, Sultan Nur al-Din ordered the construction of the first college of Hadith in Damascus. He appointed Ibn 'Asakir as its inaugural professor, a position he held until his death. It became known as *Dar al-Hadith*, which is short for *Dar al-Hadith al-Nuriyya* (Nur al-Din's College of Hadith) and also as *Dar al-Sunna* (College of the Sunna). Ibn 'Asakir had written a book to encourage Nur al-Din to construct it; it is entitled *Taqwiyat al-munna 'ala insha' dar al-sunna* (*Reinforcing the Determination to Build the College of the Sunna*), but unfortunately it is not extant.

This great reward reflected the close relationship between the scholar and the Sultan. Ibn 'Asakir not only wrote specific books, such as *al-Arba'un hadith fi al-hathth 'ala al-jihad* (addressed later in this chapter), at Nur al-Din's request, as well as finishing the *Ta'rikh Dimashq* (see Chapter 4), but he volunteered to write others and dedicated them as presents to the Sultan on specific occasions. For instance, when Nur al-Din decided to have his son al-Salih Isma'il (born 558/1163) circumcised – circumcision then was done around the age of ten – Ibn 'Asakir wrote a book on the topic of circumcision – *Tabyin al-imtinan bi-l-amr bi-l-ikhtitan* (*Proclaiming the Gratitude for God's Command of Circumcision*) – and dedicated it to the Sultan. The book comprises fourteen prophetic hadiths and eight other anecdotes and exegetical glosses by Companions or Successors, which commend the practice of circumcision and enumerate its virtues. Ibn 'Asakir later on taught the book on 5 Shawwal 569/9 May 1174 in the College of Hadith (Nur al-Din was already sick with quinsy and died six days later).

The relationship of the two went beyond the Sultan commissioning a book or the scholar dedicating a book. In his effort to endear himself to the scholars, especially in Damascus and Aleppo, Nur al-Din often attended classes with them. He sat in on a few seminars with Ibn 'Asakir, and made an effort to memorize some prophetic hadiths; at least forty of them to win the coveted divine rewards that Ibn 'Asakir mentioned to him. There were anecdotes told about Nur al-Din's dedication to learning, including one that contrasted his general demeanor as a student with that of Saladin. One such anecdote tells that once Ibn 'Asakir chastised Saladin, who was sitting in on a

Hadith seminar, for not disciplining his bodyguards who were playing in the courtyard of the College of Hadith and causing a ruckus while Ibn 'Asakir was teaching. He told Saladin that when Nur al-Din used to come to his seminars, he sat with tremendous deference because he was hearing the words of the Prophet, listened carefully, and ordered his bodyguards to sit and listen as well.

The College of Hadith was located in the neighborhood of the Gold Stone (*Hajar al-dhahab*), on the left side of the road connecting the Umayyad Mosque (to the east) and the Citadel (to the west). This street is now known as the 'Asruniyya Market (near the famous Hamidiyya Market). The building comprised a courtyard of approximately forty-nine square meters with a small fountain pool in the middle, with rooms for study and lodging around it. The main study hall (around forty-two square meters in area) was along the southern side of the building. It fell into disrepair after 804/1400, following Tamerlane's attack against Damascus. Today, only a small part of the building exists; it was renovated at the beginning of the twentieth century by a local Damascene scholar.

Ibn 'Asakir makes no mention of the College of Hadith in his *Ta'rikh*, which proves that the building had not yet been constructed by mid-winter of 559/1164 when he first taught the *Ta'rikh* (as will be discussed in Chapter 4), in which he listed the mosques and all types of prayer places in the city. In other words, had the building existed by then, he would not have neglected to list the prayer room in his own school. Therefore, 559/1164 is a *terminus post quem* for dating the College of Hadith.

The earliest reference to its existence is found in a statement at the beginning of Ibn 'Asakir's seminar on *Fadl Rajab* (*Religious Merits of the Month of Rajab*), written by his nephew Abu al-Fadl Ahmad b. Muhammad. It states that he studied the book with his uncle in the College of Hadith in two sessions: 15 and 22 Rajab 566/24 and 31 March 1171. There is also a colophon in Ibn 'Asakir's *Kashf al-mughatta 'an fadl al-Muwatta* (*Revealing the Merits of Malik's Muwatta'*) — a colophon appears at the end of a given book to identify who taught it, where it was taught, when, and who were present to study it — which states that the *Kashf* was taught by Ibn 'Asakir in the College of Hadith on Tuesday, 28 Rajab 566/6 April 1171 (Ibn 'Asakir, *Kashf al-mughatta* 49). Therefore, it is safe to date the construction of the College to sometime between spring 559/1164 and winter 566/1171, although a date closer to 566/1171 is more likely.

We do not know the full extent of Ibn 'Asakir's use of the College of Hadith for teaching and propaganda. He maintained his professorship at the Umayyad Mosque, and split his duties between both places.

The College of Hadith gained more significance in the subsequent two centuries. The chair that Ibn 'Asakir held stayed in the family, on and off, until the late seventh/thirteenth century. First, Ibn 'Asakir's son al-Qasim inherited the professorship and, after that, in 600/1203, it passed to his own son – called 'Ali (d. 616/1219), after his grandfather – and then to Ibn 'Asakir's nephew al-Hasan b. Muhammad (d. 627/1230) and his son 'Abd al-Wahhab b. al-Hasan (d. 660/1262).

After that, it passed to some of the leading scholars of Hadith in Damascus and Syria, including Jamal al-Din Ibn al-Sabuni (d. 680/1282), and Taj al-Din al-Firkah (d. 690/1291). Then, in the eighth/fourteenth century, more renowned scholars of Hadith occupied the chair, such as 'Alam al-Din al-Birzali (d. 739/1339) between 724/1324 and 739/1339 (for more on him see Chapter 4), Jamal al-Din al-Mizzi (d. 742/1341) between 739/1339 and 742/1341, Taqiy al-Din Ibn Rafi' (d. 774/1372) from 750/1349 to 774/1372, and Ibn Kathir (d. 774/1324) for three months between May and July 774/1372. Moreover, some notable scholars were known to have taught there, such as the renowned chronicler Ibn al-Athir (d. 630/1233), the famous jurist and religious activist al-'Izz Ibn 'Abd al-Salam (d. 660/1262), and the notable Hadith scholar and chronicler al-Dhahabi (d. 748/1348).

IN DEFENSE OF ASH'ARISM

As for Ibn 'Asakir's defense of Ash'arism against other Sunni rivals, it was shaped partly by his educational and dogmatic formation and also by the local Damascene rivalry between Shafi'is and

Hanbalis, which was already in place before his time. At the center was the rift between the Ash'aris and Hanbalis over theological differences, and given the fact that most Shafi'is (especially in Damascus) were Ash'aris, the fissure extended to most members of the two schools.

Controversies and animosities were very common among the competing schools of theology in Islam since the first/seventh century. In Sunnism in particular, by the end of the fourth/tenth century, four main schools of theology vied with each other, often leading to violent clashes between their adherents. They were: the Mu'tazila*, the Hanbalis, the Ash'aris, and the Maturidis*. Most often, the clashes remained contained to a specific city or area, but the Hanbali-Ash'ari animosity spread to all the places where both groups had significant followers. The Hanbalis were the only branch of jurisprudence in Sunni Islam that also had its own distinctive theological teachings and tenets. The other branches – mainly the Hanafis, Shafi'is, and Malikis* – did not have their own theology, and therefore chose from among three dominant ones: Ash'ari theology, Mu'tazila theology, or Maturidi* theology. By the sixth/twelfth century, most of the Shafi'is were Ash'aris (although at some point in the fourth/tenth and fifth/eleventh centuries, some Shafi'is adhered to Mu'tazila theology). The different schools of Sunni theology divided over some fundamental issues, most notably anthropomorphism (whether God has a human form or not), the created nature of the Qur'an, God's nature and attributes, human capacity (whether humans have free will or act according to a predestined divine plan), the role of reason vs. revelation, etc. The Hanbalis were staunch anthropomorphists, contrary to the Ash'aris who advocated that God has a shape but humans have no capacity to know it. The difference between the two was not restricted to anthropomorphism, although this seemed to be the principal issue that triggered many clashes between members of both groups in places such as Baghdad, Isfahan, and later in Damascus, especially when a theologian from one group preached or wrote about something that the other group found offensive and "heretical."

Ibn 'Asakir initially showed all indications that he could rise above the Ash'ari-Hanbali rivalry during his first educational trip to Baghdad.

There, he developed a close relationship with several renowned Hanbali teachers and was exposed to the rich diversity of Sunni views, even taking lessons on Hadith with Twelver Shi'i scholars. It must have been his second journey further east and his companionship with al-Sam'ani that cemented in his mind a negative view of the Hanbalis and turned him into an ardent defender of Sunni Ash'arism, especially when he returned to Damascus and started his official career as a scholar there. The classes he took in Baghdad on Ash'ari theology with the avid anti-Hanbali al-Isfarayini (as mentioned in Chapter 2), but also the Hanbali intimidation al-Isfarayini received there, and which Ibn 'Asakir personally witnessed, must also have soured him against them.

In his *Tabyin*, which will be covered shortly, Ibn 'Asakir repelled many of the accusations that the Hanbalis levelled against Abu al-Hasan al-Ash'ari (d. 324/936) and some Ash'ari theologians; even though the work itself was not originally meant as a refutation of them. We are also told that he used to avoid walking through the Hanbali neighborhoods for fear of harassment. Moreover, local Hanbali scholars used to avoid him and boycotted his seminars. For instance, a well-known Hanbali scholar named 'Abd al-Ghani al-Maqdisi (d. 600/1203) once asked someone to bring him a volume of Ibn 'Asakir's *Ta'rikh*. When he read it and realized its value, he regretted having missed the opportunity to study with Ibn 'Asakir due to the animosity between them (al-Dhahabi, *Siyar* 20: 568). The antagonism between the two groups lasted several centuries (and even remains in some form today), and it impacted the politics of education in Damascene society.

Nevertheless, Ibn 'Asakir's anti-Hanbali stance did not mean that he abhorred the founder of the school. To the contrary, he idealized Ahmad Ibn Hanbal (d. 241/855) and wrote a book on his fine transmission of Hadith. In this vein, Ibn 'Asakir was also very interested in the legacy of Malik b. Anas (d. 179/795), and wrote several books on the hadiths Malik purportedly transmitted, the places where Malik studied and taught Hadith, and the students who learned Hadith from him. This effort was not unrelated to his promotion of Ash'arism, given the fact that the Malikis* in Damascus followed Ash'ari theology.

Tabyin kadhib al-muftari

Ibn 'Asakir's passionate defense of Ash'arism led to the publication of his famous book *Tabyin kadhib al-muftari fi-ma nasaba ila Abi al-Hasan al-Ash'ari* (*Exposing the Slanderer's Mendacity in What He Ascribed to Abu al-Hasan al-Ash'ari*). The book was intended as a vindication of al-Ash'ari and his followers against the false accusations that were made against him, especially those levelled in the book of Abu 'Ali al-Ahwazi (d. 446/1055). Called by Ibn 'Asakir "the slanderer" (Ibn 'Asakir, *Tabyin* 35), al-Ahwazi was originally from Iraq and came to Damascus in 391/1001, where he wrote and disseminated his defamatory book against al-Ash'ari; Ibn al-'Adim of Aleppo (d. 660/1262) said that he read the book, whose title could have been *Mathalib Abi al-Hasan al-Ash'ari* (*Defects of Abu al-Hasan al-Ash'ari*) – this is inferred from indications in some of the works of Ibn Taymiyya. Al-Ahwazi was a follower of a Sunni sect called al-Salimiyya, which appeared in Basra in the fourth/tenth century and promoted anthropomorphism and mysticism; one of the school's most celebrated followers was Abu Talib al-Makki (d. 386/996), who wrote a very authoritative encyclopedia of mystical knowledge entitled *Qut al-qulub fi-mu'amalat al-mahbub* (*Nourishment of the Hearts in the Treatment of the Beloved*).

The *Tabyin* is a work of three main sections. The first section is devoted to al-Ash'ari. Here Ibn 'Asakir divulged al-Ash'ari's accomplishments and the great service he rendered to Sunnism, so much so that he considered him the renewer (*mujaddid*) of the fourth/tenth century. The idea of a renewer is based on a hadith attributed to the Prophet Muhammad, which says: "At the beginning of every century, God will send to this community a renewer who will renew its religion." Ibn 'Asakir named all the renewers in Islam who appeared at the beginning of a every century since the Prophet Muhammad: the Umayyad Caliph 'Umar b. 'Abd al-'Aziz (r. 99/717–101/720) for the second/eighth century; jurist al-Shafi'i (d. 204/820) for the third/ninth century; theologian al-Ash'ari for the fourth/tenth century; theologian al-Baqillani (d. 403/1013) for the fifth/eleventh century; and al-Ghazali for the sixth/twelfth century (Ibn 'Asakir, *Tabyin* 53). Ibn 'Asakir also emphasized the family lineage of al-Ash'ari, which he traced back to the Companion Abu Musa al-Ash'ari (d. c. 48/668), and quoted a few hadiths attributed to the Prophet Muhammad that allegedly identify the members of the Ash'ari clan as destined to play a fundamental role in the spread and future preservation of Islam.

The second section of the *Tabyin* comprises the biographies of notable Ash'aris, starting with the first generation – al-Ash'ari's companions – then subsequent generations until Ibn 'Asakir's teachers (five generations in total). The third section addresses various issues, such as theology as a permissible science and the impermissibility of vilifying fellow Muslims. He also included in this part a detailed response to the allegations of al-Ahwazi.

The book has had a very enthusiastic reception among Sunni Ash'aris in the Muslim world. The remark of al-Dhahabi sums this up very well: "Whoever seeks to develop deep knowledge about al-Ash'ari must read *Kitab Tabyin kadhib al-Muftari* by Abu al-Qasim Ibn 'Asakir" (al-Dhahabi, *Ta'rikh*, 24: 157). It was also frequently commented upon or abridged, such as the abridgment *Tabaqat al-asha'ira* (*Generations of Ash'aris*) by Ibn Imam al-Kamiliyya (d. 874/1470), who was the professor of Shafi'i law at Sultan Saladin's College, and of Hadith at Sultan al-Kamil's College, both of which were the most prestigious Sunni colleges at the time in Cairo.

The *Tabyin* also generated negative criticism, especially from some Hanbali circles who in their effort to undermine the reputation of al-Ash'ari went after Ibn 'Asakir and accused him of transmitting false hadiths and deceitfully inventing untrue reports in order to show that famous Muslim scholars were followers of the theologian. Their contention was that these scholars were against al-Ash'ari. One of those refutations – entitled *Jam' al-juyush wa-l-dasakir 'ala Ibn 'Asakir* (*Rallying the Masses and Nations against Ibn 'Asakir*) – was written by an influential Damascene Hanbali scholar named Ibn 'Abd al-Hadi al-Salihi (d. 909/1503) as an attack against Ibn 'Asakir in order to undermine his reputation and the validity of the *Tabyin*, and consequently tarnish al-Ash'ari himself.

PREACHING OF JIHAD

In the first few months of 545/1150, Ibn 'Asakir taught a seminar on the *Kitab al-Jihad* of Ibn al-Mubarak. Among his students was commander (*amir**) 'Ali b. Murshid from the powerful Banu Munqidh clan and brother of the famous Usama Ibn Munqidh (d. 584/1188). After the seminar was concluded, 'Ali departed Damascus with his brother and their troops to defend Ascalon from the army of the Second Crusade, and was killed in a battle outside the walls of Gaza, likely in Ramadan 545/December 1150. He was fifty-six years old.

There was no direct relation between the topic of the seminar and the amir's choice to fight the Crusaders, and none should be expected. The members of the Banu Munqidh clan had engaged the Franks in countless battles and skirmishes, especially around the family base in Shayzar in northwestern Syria. But their interactions with the Franks were not always hostile. In fact, that amir 'Ali studied with Ibn 'Asakir tells us more about the latter than about the former. Ibn 'Asakir was clearly involved in the preaching of jihad in Damascus. It also suggests a possible correlation between the failed attack of the Second Crusade against Damascus in the summer of 543/1148 and his becoming a jihad propagandist. The threat to his hometown could have convinced Ibn 'Asakir to write about and teach jihad. As noted earlier in Chapter 2, he had received a certificate to teach Ibn al-Mubarak's *Kitab al-Jihad* from his teacher Abu Ghalib Ibn al-Banna' in Baghdad during his first residency there.

It was not in Baghdad where Ibn 'Asakir was first exposed to jihad preaching, however. That happened in Damascus during his formative years through different forms of interactions with a group of displaced scholars who fled their villages and towns in coastal Syrian and Palestine, either because of Frankish occupation or for fear of them (as already discussed in Chapter 1). One of them was Abu al-Faraj Ghayth b. 'Ali al-Suri (d. 509/1115). He was the chief-preacher of the Friday mosque in Tyre, and left it for fear of it being captured by the Franks (the city fell to the Franks on 14 Jumada I 518/29 June 1124). Abu al-Faraj was a close friend of Ibn 'Asakir's father and lived with the 'Asakir family until his death. He taught Ibn 'Asakir hadiths on jihad. Another displaced scholar who taught Ibn 'Asakir hadiths on jihad was Abu al-Fath al-Maqdisi (d. 539/1145); he also taught him the recitation of the Qur'an. Abu al-Fath fled Jerusalem after its capture by the

Franks, and Ibn 'Asakir described him as "zealous in his advocacy for the prophetic Sunna."

It is very likely that these displaced scholars were involved in jihad preaching in Damascus for no other reason than to incite their co-religionists to rally and liberate their hometowns. The Damascene scholarly establishment, however, did not seem at first to care about that, and the Burid rulers of the city entered into an alliance with the Franks. But for Ibn 'Asakir, judging from the way he remembered these displaced scholars in the *Ta'rikh Dimsahq*, there is no doubt that they left a great impression on him. Moreover, when he wrote his *Mu'jam al-shuyukh* (*Catalogue of Teachers*) years later, he still remembered them for their jihad advocacy. Every entry in the catalogue listed the teacher's name, the town where Ibn 'Asakir met him, and a hadith that he related from him (except in very few cases where Ibn 'Asakir would list a poem instead). Each entry, therefore, helps us understand how Ibn 'Asakir remembered that particular teacher. All the hadiths on jihad, except for one in the *Mu'jam*, were related from these displaced scholars.

Therefore, one expects that when Ibn 'Asakir embarked on both of his educational journeys, he had in mind to collect hadiths on jihad and study earlier books on the topic. Indeed, evidence for this is found in the fact that during his first trip he studied *Kitab al-Jihad* of Ibn al-Mubarak, as noted earlier, and in both trips he collected several hadiths on jihad some of which he later incorporated into his treatise, entitled *al-Arba'un hadith fi al-hathth 'ala al-jihad*, as we will see below. The attack of the Second Crusade, as noted above, gave him the opportunity to take an active role in the dissemination of these hadiths and books, and to become an advocate of jihad.

Al-Arba'un hadith fi al-hathth 'ala al-jihad

The best example of Ibn 'Asakir's jihad advocacy was his treatise entitled *al-Arba'un hadith fi al-hathth 'ala al-jihad* (*Forty Hadiths for Inciting Jihad*), which he wrote at the request of Sultan Nur al-Din, as mentioned earlier. The *al-Arba'un* comprises forty hadiths attributed to the Prophet Muhammad on different aspects of jihad. Ibn 'Asakir learned them from scholars he had met during his travels, except for one case when he transmitted a hadith from two teachers: a scholar from Nishapur, and one of his leading teachers in Damascus, 'Abd al-Karim al-Sulami. Indeed, the absence of Damascene scholars from the *al-Arba'un* is surprising knowing that Ibn 'Asakir was very much exposed to hadiths on jihad in the city, as discussed earlier, and some of the ones he quoted in his work he had initially learned in Damascus from people who had a substantial impact on him. So why did he ignore Damascene and by extension Syrian scholars from the *al-Arba'un*, except for one case? A plausible explanation is that he wanted to demonstrate to Sultan Nur al-Din and to his townsfolk that he did not owe his mastery of Hadith to local teachers. Given his perception of his own worthiness vis-à-vis his contemporaries, as discussed in Chapter 2, the omission was intentional and not a coincidence.

The *al-Arba'un* was meant as a propaganda manual. The introduction gives us an idea about the motives for writing it and its intended use:

> The just king [Nur al-Din], the ascetic, the jihad fighter, and the garrisoned warrior — may God grant him success in that which is proper, assist him in fulfilling what is best for people, grant him favor against the recalcitrants, exalt him in victory with his army, and support him with aid — expressed his desire that I collect for him forty hadiths relating to jihad that have clear texts and uninterrupted sound chains of transmission so that they might stimulate the valiant jihad fighters, the ones with strong determination and mighty arms, with sharp swords and piercing spears, and stir them up to truly perform when they meet the enemy in battle, and incite them to uproot the unbelievers and tyrants who, because of their unbelief, have terrorized the land and proliferated oppression and corruption — may God pour on them all types of torture, for he is all-watching. So, I hastened to fulfill his desire and collected for him what is suitable for the people of learning and inquiry. I especially exerted a tremendous effort in collecting them in the hope that I should receive the reward [from God] for enlightening and guidance. God is the Guide to accuracy in what one initiates and completes, and the Director to right expression, be it thorough or succinct.
>
> (Ibn 'Asakir in Mourad and Lindsay, *Intensification* 132–133)

It is clear in this introduction, aside from the acknowledgment that Nur al-Din asked Ibn 'Asakir to write the book, that Ibn 'Asakir meant it for propaganda. Terms such as "stimulate," "stir", and "incite" point to it being produced as a tool to be used for rallying people to jihad rather than a scholarly exercise meant for an educated elite or a library shelf. Moreover, Ibn 'Asakir did not specifically identify the enemy against whom the jihad is to be conducted. He used oblique expressions: "unbelievers" and "tyrants," which might suggest that it was not a specific enemy he had in mind but more than one. Given the fact that in his other books he described the capture of Egypt and the demise of the Fatimid Caliphate as an accomplishment of jihad fighters, it is very plausible that he meant by the enemy here those who represented genuine threats to Nur al-Din and by extension to the project of the revival of Sunnism. As such, the enemy includes Fatimids as well as Franks, and possibly other minor rulers in Syria and northern Mesopotamia who refused to submit to Nur al-Din's rule.

A third point raised in the introduction is Ibn 'Asakir's awareness of his own role in the dissemination of jihad ideology, for it is he who is "enlightening" and providing "guidance" to the Sultan and the Muslims on this important matter, which he considered to be worthy of special divine reward.

The al-Arba'un must have been written before 7 Rajab 565/28 March 1170. This date appears in the first colophon of the unique existing complete manuscript. It states that the book was taught to family members, including Ibn 'Asakir's two sons, grandson, nephews, and maternal cousin, among others, in the family's garden in Mizza, outside Damascus. This must be seen as a special event to give the members of the family the certificate to transmit the book, and should not necessarily mean that Ibn 'Asakir finished writing it a few weeks before.

The al-Arba'un was preached in the Umayyad Mosque during the life of Ibn 'Asakir. He presided over a session on Friday, 29 Ramadan 569/3 May 1174, twelve days before Nur al-Din died. It was also used on several other occasions, especially during the time of the Fifth Crusade (615/1218–618/1221) and the Crusade of Emperor Frederick II of Hohenstaufen (625/1228–626/1229), to preach jihad in several centers around the city, including the Umayyad Mosque and the College of Hadith. Copies of it also existed in several local libraries as well, suggesting that it must have been used well in the city.

Another Book on Jihad?

Ibn 'Asakir did not write another book on jihad as it is alleged in some medieval sources. For instance, in *Siyar a'lam al-nubala'* (*Lives of Notable scholars*), al-Dhahabi listed two different titles on jihad by Ibn 'Asakir: *Kitab al-Jihad* and *al-Arba'un hadith fi al-hathth 'ala al-jihad*. This, however, is a mistake. Ibn 'Asakir only wrote the latter, never the former. The mistake resulted from a misreading of two lists of books that Ibn 'Asakir's son al-Qasim had compiled, and which are preserved in the *Mu'jam al-udaba'* by Yaqut al-Hamawi. The first list gives the titles of the books that al-Qasim knew his father wrote, and which includes the *Forty hadiths*. The second list identifies other titles that al-Qasim surmised his father had started or intended to write but never finished. This second list includes *Kitab Fadl al-jihad* (*On the Merits of Jihad*) and a title on *Fadl al-Bayt al-Muqaddas* (*Merits of Jerusalem*). Al-Qasim wrote a book on jihad for Sultan Saladin and another one on the merits of Jerusalem entitled *al-Mustaqsa fi fada'il al-masjid al-aqsa* (*The Exhaustive Treatise on the Merits of the Aqsa Sanctuary*). One should not assume that these were originally written by the father, but it could be that al-Qasim partly based his own works on projects his father had started or thought to write but never did.

RELIGIOUS MERITS OF TOWNS AND PLACES

Another category of works that help us understand Ibn 'Asakir's scholarship and activism is that relating to the religious merits of towns and places in and around Damascus. This interest was reflective of a tremendous sense of pride or love of the homeland he had as a Damascene and Syrian, something he shared with many there. It might be considered a kind of medieval patriotism that also shaped identity and defined belonging in premodern Islamic times.

The literature on the religious merits (*fada'il*) of a given place was very popular in medieval Islam, and many books were written on the subject. The two most popular cities that received the largest attention were Jerusalem and Mecca. Syria (*Bilad al-Sham*) also received some attention, largely thanks to the advocacy of Syrian scholars. The introductory volume of Ibn 'Asakir's *Ta'rikh* give us many examples of the kind of traditions and anecdotes scholars in Syria circulated about the religious merits of their land, towns, and sacred shrines, which leave no doubt about the seminal role Ibn 'Asakir and many of his townsmen thought their hometown and Syria played in God's past, present, and future designs. The following three hadiths give us an idea of that:

> Thawr b. Yazid (d. c. 153/770) said: "The holiest part of earth is Syria, the holiest part of Syria is Palestine, the holiest part of Palestine is Jerusalem, the holiest part of Jerusalem is the Temple Mount, the holiest part of the Temple Mount is the Sanctuary, and the holiest part of the Sanctuary is the Dome of the Rock."
>
> (Ibn 'Asakir, *Ta'rikh* 1: 152)

> The Messenger of God, may God praise and bless him, said: "Good is ten portions, nine are in Syria and one is in the rest of the world. Evil is ten portions, one is in Syria and nine are in the rest of the world. When the people of Syria become corrupt, there is no hope."
>
> (Ibn 'Asakir, *Ta'rikh* 1: 154)

> The Messenger of God, may God praise and bless him, said: "All regions of the world will be destroyed forty years before Syria."
>
> (Ibn 'Asakir, *Ta'rikh* 1: 194)

These three hadiths, and many others like them that we find in the *Ta'rikh*, help us understand how Ibn 'Asakir thought of the unique role Syria played in salvation history, which necessitated that its inhabitants measure up to divine expectations of them. Thus, he assumed the role of the reviver of memory about the distinction and religious merits of his hometown and its environs. These places ooze with sanctity and religious merits because of the divine events and personalities associated with them in the past and those destined to unfold in the future. This divine history stretched from biblical times and extended all the way to the events that will usher the Day of Judgment (for more on this, see Chapter 4).

The other merit that Damascus and its environs possess in God's divine plan is the role of the local scholars in the transmission of Hadith. By transmitting the Sunna of the Prophet, they helped preserve the central pillar of Islam that holds the religion together. Thus, aside from the *Ta'rikh*, Ibn 'Asakir authored twenty-seven treatises on Hadith scholars and the hadiths they transmitted; these scholars hailed from numerous villages and towns around Damascus, such as Darayya, Mizza, Kafar Susa, San'a', al-Nayrab, Ba'labakk, and so on. In other words, it is as if Ibn 'Asakir were saying that the transmission of Hadith in those towns and the residency of Hadith scholars there blessed those places. Moreover, he considered such information the only history worth documenting about those places. In other words, if we examine the books he wrote about them – those that have survived – we only find very short biographies of Hadith transmitters and the hadiths they related. We find nothing else.

Fadl 'Asqalan

Ibn 'Asakir also wrote a book entitled *Fadl 'Asqalan (Merits of Ascalon)*. It is possible that it was compiled around the time the army of the Second Crusade attacked and captured the city in 548/1153, either as an appeal for the Muslims to protect it or to liberate it. The book contains hadiths and other traditions about the distinction of Ascalon for Islam and the notable Muslims who lived and died there. It is lost, although the hadiths that he cited in it could have been preserved in a manuscript containing an abridgment of al-Qasim's *al-Mustaqsa*.

IBN 'ASAKIR AS THEOLOGIAN AND HISTORIAN

Was Ibn 'Asakir a Theologian?

Was Ibn 'Asakir a theologian? This is an important question given the fact that some today might think of him as a theologian on account of a few books he wrote, especially the *Tabyin* in which he defended the famous theologian al-Ash'ari and the Ash'ari school. This, however, has no foundation in fact. Ibn 'Asakir was not a theologian and in none of his writings do we find him employing the language and vocabulary that we typically associate with theologians (*mutakallimun*).

Take, for example, his book *Fi nafi al-tashbih* (*Against Anthropomorphism*), which was the subject of his seminar no. 138. Ibn 'Asakir related six prophetic hadiths which report that when the Prophet Muhammad was asked by his followers or others (including Christians, Jews, and Meccan polytheists) to describe to them God, his reply was always: "Say God is One," which is the first verse of Qur'an 112 (*Surat al-Ikhlas* or True Devotion). He also related a seventh hadith about a polytheist ruler who was invited to convert to Islam but insisted that the Prophet describe to him first whether God was made of silver or brass, and because of his insistence God sent against him a lightning bolt that killed him. Ibn 'Asakir concluded his treatise on anthropomorphism with a hadith attributed to Ibn 'Abbas, and three other anecdotes, two taken from the *Risala* (*Epistle*) of al-Qushayri (d. 465/1072) and attributed to the famous mystics al-Hallaj (d. 309/922) and al-Sarraj (d. 378/988), and one taken from Abu Nu'aym al-Isfahani (d. 430/1038) and attributed to Hadith scholar Abu Ishaq Ibrahim b. Hamza b. 'Imara (d. 353/964), who said:

> I profess that whoever described the exalted and glorious God by comparing him to his creation, or believed in his heart that he is in the form of a beardless youth, I consider him an unbeliever.
>
> (Ibn 'Asakir, *Fi nafi al-tashbih* 57)

This view, which Abu Nu'aym quoted in one of his works that did not survive, is specifically telling, for he had a history of trouble with the Hanbalis in Isfahan, and they conspired to kill him several times and once banned him from teaching in the city's main mosque. It shows that Abu Nu'aym indeed endorsed the view that those who adhere to anthropomorphism are unbelievers, which was one of the major sticking points between the Ash'aris and Hanbalis, thus corroborating what later scholars said about him, that he was an Ash'ari. The view that God looks like a beardless boy is based on a hadith attributed to the Prophet – who allegedly said: "I saw my Lord in the most beautiful form; a beardless youth with long curly hair, wearing a green robe" – which some Hanbalis used to transmit (such as in Ibn Abu Ya'la al-Farra', *Tabaqat al-hanabila* 2: 46).

Ibn 'Asakir concluded his seminar on anthropomorphism, as in all his other seminars and most of his books, with a short poem by one of his teachers featuring the following line:

> Cursed is the insolent who says that God is
> a body and that our features are like his features.

All of this indicates that Ibn 'Asakir must have shared these views. Nevertheless, nowhere in *Fi nafi al-tashbih* do we find Ibn 'Asakir expressing his own views on the issue of anthropomorphism or analyzing the material he was quoting. Similarly, in the *Tabyin* he reported hadiths, anecdotes, and views expressed by Ash'ari scholars, but we do not find his own voice on controversial theological issues. This does not mean, however, that he was not educated in theology or possibly could have expressed theological views in informal settings. What it does mean is that we do not find such views expressed in his writings, and we do not see any command on his part of theological language and vocabulary independently of what he cited. It is therefore reasonable that he should not be considered or called a theologian.

Was Ibn 'Asakir a Historian?

The question of whether we can call Ibn 'Asakir a historian is somewhat similar to the earlier discussion about whether we can call him a theologian, but with a major difference. He was a classical scholar who wrote and thought about history in the way many in his day did as well. That is, Ibn 'Asakir was concerned with recounting history through the preservation and transmission of anecdotes about the lives and scholarly biographies of those (men and women) who had an impact (specifically a moral impact) on Islam and its people – biblical prophets and personalities, the Prophet Muhammad and his Companions, Muslim rulers, fellow scholars, etc. – not through the prism of rigid annals and chronology. As such, while Ibn 'Asakir was not a chronicler or what we might consider a traditional historian, he was very much concerned with a proper understanding of the Islamic past – the history that mattered.

Take for example the biography of Nur al-Din, which covers six and a half pages in the modern Dar al-Fikr edition of the *Ta'rikh*. What we see there is not chronicled history. The biography was written during the lifetime of Nur al-Din, and has a feature that we do not encounter in other biographies in the *Ta'rikh*, namely a very refined rhymed prose, which clearly reflects a conscious effort on the part of Ibn 'Asakir to please his political patron. Nevertheless, it was more a religious eulogy than a traditional historical biography. For instance, Ibn 'Asakir listed all the places that Nur al-Din conquered, but he did not give dates for these conquests. Similarly, Ibn 'Asakir enumerated the cities in which Nur al-Din ordered the construction of hospitals and Sufi dwellings, but he did not specify which buildings he endowed in each city or the date of their respective construction. He tallied the Sultan's benevolences, but one fails to find any specifics about them. Even regarding the most important accomplishment of Nur al-Din, which according to Ibn 'Asakir was the jihad against the Franks, he did not chronicle any battles and the two campaigns against Antioch he referenced lack specific details that a traditional historian would have included.

Similarly, the biography of Abu Hamid al-Ghazali teaches us nothing about his residency and activities in Damascus or his impact on religious education in the city. It tells us nothing about the students who crammed the northwestern corner of the Umayyad Mosque compound to study with al-Ghazali, and which became known in Ibn 'Asakir's day as the *Zawiya* of al-Ghazali. Ibn 'Asakir lifted the biography in its entirety – except for a few basic lines about the year al-Ghazali was born and the year he died – from the *Dhayl Ta'rikh Naysabur* (*Continuation of the History of Nishapur*) of Abu al-Hasan al-Farisi (d. 529/1135), who had sent Ibn 'Asakir a certificate to transmit the book and died two months before Ibn 'Asakir arrived in Nishapur. Clearly, Ibn 'Asakir thought al-Farisi's eulogy of al-Ghazali was the best that could be written about the exemplary scholar. What is surprising is that Ibn 'Asakir knew an enormous amount of

information about al-Ghazali's sojourns in Damascus from his rela-
tives and teachers. We find this information scattered, in no organized
manner, all over the Ta'rikh Dimsahq, but not where it mattered most:
in the biography of al-Ghazali.

Equally, the biography of the Burid ruler of Damascus Abaq, whose
reign overlapped with an active portion of Ibn 'Asakir's career, provides meager information about his time in Damascus, and we find no
mention whatsoever of the most important event that unfolded during
his tenure: the attack of the army of the Second Crusade against the
city in Rabi' I 543/July 1148. We also do not find a biography of
Mu'in al-Din Unur in the Ta'rikh, even though his influence in the history of Damascus and Syria was immense, and is credited with endowing the Mu'iniyya College (as mentioned in Chapter 1), and which Ibn
'Asakir knew well.

Even if we look at the two introductory volumes on Damascus,
they do not furnish any chronology or survey the history of the city.
There are aspects of the city's history (though none for his own time)
that he retold through historical anecdotes, hadiths, and legends, but
they are not arranged in a timeline or sequential order.

This is the approach to historical writing Ibn 'Asakir adopted in
all his writings. The word Ta'rikh for him is not really history in the
traditional sense of chronology and annals, it is rather documentation.
Therefore, one should not think of him as a historian in the traditional
sense of a chronicler, like for instance his contemporary and towns-
man Ibn al-Qalanisi (d. 555/1160) who wrote what is known as Dhayl
Ta'rikh Dimashq (A Short Survey of the History of Damascus), and which is
a traditional chronicle (for more on the Dhayl, see Chapter 4). He was
not like al-Dhahabi, who blended the two styles (chronology and biography) in his Ta'rikh al-Islam. Nor can we compare him to al-Tabari
(d. 310/923), who narrated history through anecdotes and quotations
from prior sources, although his collage offered a vast chronological
history of Islam (including some aspects of pre-Islamic times).

The view that Ibn 'Asakir was a historian with modern insinua-
tions became widespread in the twentieth century, when he started
being referred to as mu'arrikh al-sham, meaning the historian who
documented the history of Damascus and Syria (on the modernists'

utilization of Ibn 'Asakir, see Chapter 7). It is more proper, as argued earlier, to treat Ibn 'Asakir as a historian who wrote about and thought of history as many in his day did but not as modern historians do. He was the kind of historian who crafted his vision of the Islamic past via individual anecdotes about persons — scholars, sacred figures, rulers, etc. — and places that shaped the history of Islam. As such, his approach makes his books, especially the *Ta'rikh*, repositories of some indispensable raw historical data that are of tremendous value for modern historians.

TA'RIKH DIMASHQ

The *Ta'rikh Dimashq* is Ibn 'Asakir's magnum opus. The full title is *Ta'rikh madinat Dimashq wa-dhikr fadliha wa-tasmiyat man hallaha min al-amathil aw ijtaz bi-nawahiha min waridiha wa-ahliha* (*History of the City of Damascus and the Mention of Its Merits, with Identification of Those Who Lived in It from among the Exemplars or Those Who Passed by or Lived in Its Environs*). Its sheer size reveals the enormous effort he put into writing it, and anyone who reads it is awed by the massive knowledge Ibn 'Asakir had acquired. It assured him a legacy in Islam that very few scholars could attain. It became a foundational reference on the history of Damascus and Syria and on Hadith, and remains so until today, and it inspired many writers to produce something comparable, though much shorter in size. It was also used in the creation of modern Syrian national identity and historical memory in the twentieth century (as will be discussed in Chapter 7).

THE IDEA

Ibn 'Asakir must have conceptualized the project of the *Ta'rikh* before he embarked on his second educational trip in 529/1135. We have some clues that indicate he was already thinking about it during his first educational sojourns in Baghdad, and benefitted from the many encounters he had there to collect the necessary sources he needed for the project. He said, for instance, that his teacher Abu al-Fadl al-Hafiz handed him a copy of *Kitab Ishtiqaq asma' al-buldan* (*On the Origins of Place Names*) of Abu al-Husayn Ibn Faris, and he later on quoted from it in the introductory section of the *Ta'rikh* when discussing the origins of the terms *al-Sham* (Syria) and *Dimashq* (Damascus), among others. This suggests that Ibn 'Asakir must have discussed the project with Abu al-Fadl al-Hafiz, which prompted the latter to point him to a valuable source. Ibn 'Asakir also mentioned that he had started working on the *Ta'rikh* to his travel companion al-Sam'ani at the time when the two met in 529/1135. This information is corroborated by Ibn 'Asakir himself in the introduction to the *Ta'rikh* where he said that back in the day when he was young, he had started making a history for the city of Damascus, but the years went by and other concerns interfered causing its delay.

It is very likely that Ibn 'Asakir came up with the idea to write the *Ta'rikh* when he first studied *Ta'rikh Baghdad* of al-Khatib al-Baghdadi, and wanted to produce something similar for his hometown. *Ta'rikh Baghdad* was one of the first works Ibn 'Asakir had studied in Damascus as a young pupil. Moreover, he must have heard a lot about al-Khatib al-Baghdadi from his local teachers and idolized him, for they came to know him well when he resided and taught for eight years in the city (451/1059–459/1065) following his escape from Baghdad. Some even followed him to Tyre when he moved there between early 459/1065 and late 462/1070. As discussed in Chapter 1, al-Khatib al-Baghdadi brought a high level of expertise in Hadith and other subjects that the Sunnis in Syria lacked at the time. A few decades later, al-Ghazali made a similar impact, and the Damascenes remembered both visits for centuries. Living under the shadow of Shi'ism depleted and marginalized Sunnism in Syria and Egypt, and exacerbated Sunni scholars' need for the high literature and expertise of Sunni scholars in Iraq, Iran, and beyond. This gradually changed in the course of the sixth/twelfth century, but when Ibn 'Asakir was still a young student those visitors from the East were among his idols.

There were other scholars who wrote a history for Damascus but they did not serve as the model for Ibn 'Asakir. His older contemporary Ibn al-Qalanisi wrote what is known as *Dhayl Ta'rikh Dimashq*, which chronicles events between 363/974 and 555/1160. The *Dhayl*, however, does not share anything with Ibn 'Asakir's *Ta'rikh* in terms of style, scope, or coverage, and therefore could not have been a model for it. Incidentally, the idea that Ibn al-Qalanisi's *Dhayl* was a continuation of Ibn 'Asakir's *Ta'rikh*, as some scholars might repeat, is totally absurd. One can even speculate that the absence of a work on Damascus similar to that of al-Khatib al-Baghdadi on Baghdad was one of the factors that motivated Ibn 'Asakir to begin composing one.

Nevertheless, it was the patronage of Sultan Nur al-Din that prompted Ibn 'Asakir to earnestly complete his project and start disseminating it. In the prologue, Ibn 'Asakir informed his readers that the word had spread that he was writing a book on the history of Damascus and many colleagues came inquiring about its progress or asked to study it, which caused him some embarrassment. Finally, Nur al-Din inquired about it and urged Ibn 'Asakir to finish it in order to get a chance to read it (we do not know whether someone prompted the Sultan to do so or he simply got word of it and was curious to learn about its status). Ibn 'Asakir obliged and the *Ta'rikh* was complete by early Rabi' II 559/late February 1164.

It should be noted that it was actually the heroic efforts of Ibn 'Asakir's son al-Qasim, who transcribed the massive *Ta'rikh* into its final clean copy, which allowed for its dissemination from 559/1164 onward; he also produced an expanded version (addressed later in this chapter). Al-Dhahabi said the following about al-Qasim's contribution:

> If it were not for his transcription of the *Ta'rikh* and copying it from the rough draft, the great scholar – meaning his father – would not have been able to refine it and fix its language. For when he [Ibn 'Asakir] finished the rough draft, he was incapable of transcribing it himself, fixing its language, correcting its errors and setting its layout because his eyesight became weak.
>
> (al-Dhahabi, *Siyar* 21: 410)

Al-Dhahabi added that al-Qasim was not allowed to attend the teaching sessions that Ibn 'Asakir held to disseminate the book until he completed the transcription (for this, we actually have evident proof in the manuscript tradition, as we will see below). There were even rumors that the father and son did not speak to each other for some time because of this issue, and that Ibn 'Asakir vowed not to talk to his son until he finished transcribing the clean copy. The old man, nonetheless, used to confide to some of his friends that if it were not for al-Qasim, "the *Ta'rikh* would never have been finished."

THE BOOK

The *Ta'rikh* is a massive book, probably better called an encyclopedia, even an archive that preserves thousands of quotations from works that would not have survived otherwise. It is both a biographical dictionary and gigantic repository of Hadith and historical accounts. It comprises around 10,500 biographies. Almost each biography contains at least one if not many hadiths (around 15,000 in total), which was a major criterion, sometimes the sole criterion that Ibn 'Asakir used when assessing the worthiness of a person for inclusion in his book.

The *Ta'rikh* is a work that has a strong religious agenda, and Ibn 'Asakir intended it to celebrate the centrality of Syria and Damascus to Islam and even God's involvement with humanity there. It is important to remind ourselves here that it was written at a time when the region witnessed an internal power struggle among Muslims and external attacks, especially the Crusader invasion.

The first two volumes present a selective survey of the history and religious significance of Damascus and Syria, including quite a few hadiths recording what the Prophet Muhammad supposedly said about them. He also included a large number of local legends about Damascus that connected the city and Syria to several biblical events and the trials of the Day of Judgment. Examples include biblical legends and prophetic traditions about the Grotto of Blood where the locals allege Cain slayed his brother Abel (as mentioned in Chapter 2), Bayt Lihya as the town where, apparently, biblical Abraham lived and destroyed the idols, and al-Rabwa (on the northwestern outskirts of Damascus) where Mary and Jesus purportedly sought refuge from the Massacre of the Innocents by King Herod (Matthew 2.16).

Ibn 'Asakir featured as well a sketch on the Islamic conquests, the history of the Umayyad Mosque and some highlights of Umayyad projects in Damascus, a list of the city's mosques and prayer places, its churches, its rivers and waterways, its gates, and cemeteries. All of this material came in the form of anecdotes, which he quoted from his sources. Each anecdote is preceded by a chain of transmission, a medieval form of referencing indicating how it was transmitted from person to person, starting with the one who allegedly uttered it up to Ibn 'Asakir. In other words, Ibn 'Asakir takes a semi-active role in that he reported these anecdotes as he found them in his sources. Yet, he had the exclusive say on what to select from his sources and how to arrange the anecdotes in ways to make the most impact on his readers.

He also included a large number of apocalyptic narratives about the circumstances surrounding the end times and the Day of Resurrection (the name preferred by most Muslim authors to mean the Day of Judgment; that is, the time when the dead are resurrected for the final judgment). One fascinating legend he cited, and which remains very popular among the Damascenes, is that Jesus' return to this world will take place first in Damascus; he will descend atop the White Minaret (also known as the Minaret of Jesus) above the eastern side of the Umayyad Mosque.

The remaining volumes contain the biographies of notable men and women who lived in the city and its surroundings or passed through it from early Islamic times to Ibn 'Asakir's day. He also included a number of biblical figures (e.g., Abraham, Sarah, David, Solomon, Mary, John the Baptist, Jesus, Jesus' disciples) to further show God's involvement in Syria from the beginning of times and the divine attention that favored this particular spot of land over all others.

The Ta'rikh, therefore, conveys a clear sense of attachment to place, a medieval patriotism that is not associated with a nation-state but rather with a geography. Moreover, it is not to be seen as a work of history in the traditional sense. It provides no chronology whatsoever, and its discussion of events is very selective and unorganized. We cannot compare it to Ibn al-Qalanisi's Dhayl Ta'rikh Dimashq mentioned earlier, which is a classical chronicle. We cannot even compare it to al-Dhahabi's Ta'rikh al-islam (History of Islam), which is divided according to decades and each volume contains both a chronological sketch at the beginning, followed by biographies according to the year of death.

When the *Ta'rikh* is described as a biographical dictionary, this is to be understood in a broad sense in that the biographies are generally shaped in the following manner: the full name of the person, date of birth if known, education and teaching activities, date of death if known, and some hadiths. In some cases, we find additional historical accounts about that person such as certain events they witnessed or in which they were involved, their travels, etc. In this respect, the significance of most figures (including political patrons) was often portrayed in terms of the hadiths they narrated. In other words, a major factor that elevated their worthiness was by being trustees of the Prophet's teachings (*Sunna*).

It is important to clarify, however, that the *Ta'rikh* was not a prosopography (a catalogue of people who shared the same profession). It does not tell us only about transmitters of Hadith who lived in Damascus. Ibn 'Asakir made an enormous effort to include, as he put it in the introduction, all "exemplary people who resided in it or passed by it and its environs, who were virtuous and of high esteem, from among its prophets, exemplars, Caliphs, rulers, jurists, judges, scholars, luminaries, Qur'an reciters, grammarians, poets, and Hadith transmitters..."

Nevertheless, Ibn 'Asakir listed many hadiths that were known to be weak or questionable, or featured transmitters accused of being liars and falsifiers of hadith accounts. He must have known that he was taking a major risk; and later scholars pointed this out, such as al-Dhahabi, who accused Ibn 'Asakir of transmitting weak hadiths (as will be discussed in Chapter 6). The nature of hadiths that celebrate the religious merits of specific places in the Muslim world were generally transmitted by minor Hadith scholars or were suspicious reports to start with. Given his extensive study and intricate knowledge of the sciences of Hadith, especially the books about its transmitters and their trustworthiness, there is no way to argue that he did not know of the questionable nature of countless hadith reports he cited throughout the *Ta'rikh*. Sometimes, he would surprisingly say outright that a hadith he just quoted was false. However, in order to write the history of Damascus and its area in a way to make it the center of God's plan, Ibn 'Asakir's task required that he use these questionable reports that attest to major historical figures living, and events unfolding, in and around Damascus.

At any rate, in the *Ta'rikh* Ibn 'Asakir created a new historical memory for the city of Damascus and by extension for Syria. It was not its novelty inasmuch as its massive size that was unprecedented. We rarely encounter his direct voice; nevertheless, he let the thousands of carefully selected hadiths, historical accounts, anecdotes, and legends speak for him, and he deployed them craftily throughout his *Ta'rikh* in order to achieve his objectives. As argued earlier, the religious-historical memory he designed extended backwards to the beginning of creation and foreword to the end of times, thus making Damascus and Syria the central scene in God's involvement with humanity. Moreover, it was an Islamic memory, in that the present, past, and future, in Ibn 'Asakir's construction, were being harnessed as a testimony of Islam's superiority, in particular Sunni Islam, as the true religion of God. Hence, Adam, Abraham, Sarah, Mary, Jesus, even Jesus' disciples were all portrayed as Muslims, and they were even "deployed" not only to vindicate Islam but also to delegitimize their historical followers. The same was applied to some Shi'i imams as we will see below.

Rehabilitation of Past Figures and Islamic Unity

Like many scholars of his time, Ibn 'Asakir read history backward, extending Sunni genealogy all the way to the Prophet and even rehabilitating some problematic figures so that they could occupy their prestigious place in Sunni religious and scholarly ancestry. Indeed, one of the major features of the *Ta'rikh* is the effort Ibn 'Asakir exerted to rehabilitate problematic historical figures and also include personalities revered by groups Ibn 'Asakir considered heretical or wayward. The goal was to convey a sense of unity among the Muslims, which was evidently tied to Ibn 'Asakir's advocacy for the revivification of Sunnism (on this see Chapter 3) and not a real attempt to bridge the divide and bring everyone under the same roof.

Caliph Yazid b. Mu'awiya (r. 60/680–64/683) is probably the best case to illustrate how Ibn 'Asakir rehabilitated problematic historical

figures so that they could find their place among Syria's Islamic pedigree. Yazid's legacy in Sunni Islam – not to mention his satanic portrait in Shi'ism – is problematic to say the least, partly because he was
responsible for the killing of Imam al-Husayn (d. 61/680) and partly
because his personal conduct was anything but exemplary (Yazid was
known for his drinking habits and lack of responsibility). Ibn 'Asakir
rehabilitated him by focusing on three traits: Yazid's transmission of
prophetic hadiths, jihad campaigns against the Byzantines, and leading
the pilgrimage caravan to Mecca. Other scholars would have avoided
Yazid altogether, but not Ibn 'Asakir. For him, and despite Yazid's
many shortcomings, all of which were clearly known to Ibn 'Asakir,
he was an important brick in the Sunni edifice that Ibn 'Asakir was
creating for Damascus and Syria. The three traits helped Ibn 'Asakir
portray a Yazid who was eager to defend Islam, preserve the prophetic
traditions, and help the Muslims fulfil their most important religious
obligations. To make his portrait effective, Ibn 'Asakir used weak and
false prophetic hadiths and questionable historical anecdotes.

With respect to inclusion, Ibn 'Asakir featured biographies for
several Shi'i imams, their sons and daughters who lived in Syria, and
some of whom were buried in and around Damascus. For example, he
composed a very long biography (150 pages) for Imam al-Husayn. He
started it with a very stunning claim: "He (Husayn) came to congrat-
ulate Mu'awiya, and joined a jihad campaign to Constantinople which
was led by Yazid b. Mu'awiya" (Ibn 'Asakir, *Ta'rikh* 14: 111). Like so
many of the reports in this biography, they were very suspicious and
often labeled by other scholars as pure fabrications. Yet, Ibn 'Asakir
insisted on citing them, hoping that his audience would ignore their
fraudulence and accept their content. A stellar case is the following
anecdote:

> Once, al-Husayn came to see Mu'awiya b. Abu Sufyan. He arrived
> on Friday while Mu'awiya was standing on the pulpit delivering a
> sermon. A person in the crowd said: "O Commander of the Faithful,
> invite al-Husayn b. 'Ali to join you on the pulpit?" Mu'awiya replied:
> "Be quiet, let me have my moment of pride." He praised and thanked
> God, then said: "I beseech you, O Abu 'Abd Allah, am I not the son of
> the plain-valley of Mecca." Al-Husayn retorted: "Indeed you are, and I

swear to that by the one who sent my grandfather to reveal the truth."
Mu'awiya then said: "By God, O Abu 'Abd Allah, I ask you: 'Am I not
the maternal-uncle of the believers?' Al-Husayn replied: "Indeed you
are, and I swear to that by the one who sent my grandfather as prophet."
Mu'awiya then said: "By God, O Abu 'Abd Allah, I ask you: 'Am I not
the one who wrote down the revelation?'" Al-Husayn replied: "Indeed
you are, and I swear to that by the one who sent my grandfather as
forewarner." Then Mu'awiya stepped down from the pulpit and al-
Husayn b. 'Ali ascended to it. He thanked the almighty and glorious
God in ways not used by people before or after. Afterwards, he said:
"My father ['Ali] told me from my grandfather [Prophet Muhammad]
from Gabriel, peace on him, from almighty and glorious God who said:
'Under the foot of the throne, there is a green leaf of myrtle, on which
it is written: There is no god but God, Muhammad is the messenger
of God, O followers of Muhammad's family, every one of you who
comes on the Day of Resurrection saying "There is no god but God,"
God will admit him to Paradise.'" Mu'awiya b. Abu Sufyan asked: "By
God, O Abu 'Abd Allah, I ask you to explain who are the followers of
Muhammad's family?" He replied: "They are those who do not curse the
two venerable elders Abu Bakr and 'Umar, who do not curse 'Uthman,
who do not curse my father, and who do not curse you, O Mu'awiya."

(Ibn 'Asakir, *Ta'rikh* 14: 113–114)

By "maternal-uncle of the believers," Mu'awiya meant that his sister
Umm Habiba was married to the Prophet. Mu'awiya also enumerated
his other merits: being a true member of Quraysh (the tribe of Mecca)
and one of the scribes who allegedly the Prophet Muhammad asked to
write down the revelation that he received. Anyway, it is clear that Ibn
'Asakir's intention for reporting this fake anecdote was to distinguish
the Imam al-Husayn from his Shi'i followers, given the fact that he is
the most central figure of Shi'ism. This has a special importance in a
city like Damascus that in Ibn 'Asakir's day featured a large community of Shi'is, some of whose notables were converting to Sunnism,
such as one of Ibn 'Asakir's most renowned teachers Abu al-Qasim
al-Nasib, whose lineage is traced all the way back to Imam al-Husayn.
For them, Sunnism might be the way for the future, but figures like
al-Husayn were part and parcel of their family fabric, and Ibn 'Asakir
was eager to validate that.

Ibn 'Asakir also knew very well that the divine hadith (*hadith qudsi*) he related about al-Husayn, and which is embedded in the anecdote quoted above, was a fake one; divine hadiths are the most authoritative class of hadiths as they feature God as the direct speaker. So, the question that one poses is why did Ibn 'Asakir relate it if it was fake (and he did acknowledge it as fake)? The answer is that like most of the material in his *Ta'rikh* that deals with sacredness and problematic issues, he wanted the hadiths and traditions to be correct because of the messages they convey, and without them he could not make his case and "resolve" very problematic episodes in Islamic history.

In a similar way, Ibn 'Asakir's biography of Jesus and that of Jesus' disciples are telling with respect to his effort to reconcile historical issues. He was eager to vindicate Jesus and his disciples from any role in perpetrating the kinds of "heresies" that Christians came to believe about his divinity. As such, both Jesus and his disciples were made by Ibn 'Asakir into exemplars of pure Islam, which was the religion of all biblical prophets, patriarchs, and matriarchs.

The fundamental belief in the return of Jesus at the End of Times is a hallmark of Ibn 'Asakir's portraits of him. Here as well, Damascus features in this scenario in the same way it played a role as the place of refuge for the holy family. According to several hadiths and anecdotes Ibn 'Asakir cited, and which remain popular among the Damascenes, Jesus will first descend, as mentioned earlier, atop the White Minaret on the eastern side of the Umayyad Mosque. From there, he will victoriously lead the Muslims in the apocalyptic battle against the Antichrist, after which human existence in this world comes to an end with the Day of Resurrection/Judgment.

Arrangement and Divisions

Ibn 'Asakir arranged the *Ta'rikh* in the following order. The first two volumes, as mentioned earlier, were dedicated to the description of Damascus and its environs, which included some narratives about the Islamic conquests of Syria and about the religious merits of many spots and structures in the city and in its vicinity. He then designated the two following volumes for the Prophet Muhammad. After that, he arranged the biographies according to the Arabic alphabet, starting with the letter *aleph* (A) and ending with the letter *ya'* (Y). Under each letter, he listed the biographies in alphabetical order, though for the letters A and M he started with those named Ahmad and Muhammad respectively because of their honor of place, being the names of the Prophet. He did the same with the category of names 'Abd, where he started with 'Abd Allah because Allah is the name of God, whereas the others are his epithets. Following that, Ibn 'Asakir earmarked three volumes for those men who were only known through an honorific or nickname, or were unknown except for being mentioned in some sources as having lived or passed through Damascus and Syria. Finally, the last two volumes were designated for women of various social and religious importance.

There were two divisions of the *Ta'rikh*. The original division, which partitioned the text into 570 fascicles, and the expanded division, which divided it into 800 fascicles. The latter was prepared by al-Qasim during the lifetime of his father and under his supervision, but he only circulated it after his father had died. Indeed, we find confirmation about the two divisions in the short biography that al-Qasim did for his father, which is preserved in Yaqut al-Hamawi's *Mu'jam al-udaba'*, where he mentioned both versions. They are also attested in the different manuscripts of the *Ta'rikh* where we find mention of both divisions, sometimes simultaneously in the same manuscript, in the colophons about the various teaching sessions held to disseminate the text, the locations where they occurred, and the names of those who were in attendance. For instance, a note in one manuscript (volume 63 in Dar al-Fikr edition) specifies the text as coming from fascicles 502–509 of the original division, whereas another remark in another manuscript (volume 62 in the same edition) associates the text with fascicles 701–710, which formed volume 71 of the expanded division.

This is further corroborated by 'Imad al-Din al-Isfahani who said in his *Kharidat al-qasr* that he saw a copy of the *Ta'rikh* shortly after his arrival in Damascus in 562/1166, and asked Ibn 'Asakir to teach him a few parts from it. He stated that Ibn 'Asakir told him the book reached 700 fascicles, each containing 20 folios. This actually gives us a relatively specific dating as to when work on the expanded version started. If we understand that the shorter version was first circulated in 559/1164 (as discussed below), and Ibn 'Asakir showed 'Imad al-Din al-Isfahani an unfinished version of 700 fascicles in 562/1166, then the work on the expanded version must have started around 560/1165.

There has been a confusion about the two divisions, and it is not always clear when examining a manuscript of the *Ta'rikh* to which division it belongs. Although, it seems that almost all of them are based on the expanded version; the notes in the manuscripts that indicate where a fascicle ends match the expanded version, not the original. The confusion is partly caused by misreading the transmission notes in the book and the colophons at the end. It is important to point out that most existing manuscripts where we find information about the transmission of the *Ta'rikh* are traceable to one common source: Muhammad b. Yusuf al-Birzali (d. 636/1239), a scholar who came from Seville and inhabited Damascus from 610/1213 (for more on him, see Chapter 6). Al-Birzali started making his own copy of the *Ta'rikh* – the version of 800 fascicles – in 612/1215 and finished it in 617/1220. But to teach and transmit the *Ta'rikh* to others, he needed a certificate. Thus, he started in Dhu al-Qa'da 614/February 1218 with some of the students of Ibn 'Asakir. But he was eager for more prestigious certificates. For that, he turned to more important students of Ibn 'Asakir, namely his two nephews al-Hasan b. Muhammad and 'Abd al-Rahman b. Muhammad (for more on them see Chapter 5), and Abu Nasr Ibn al-Shirazi (549/1155–635/1238). Between 616/1221 and 620/1223, al-Birzali read the *Ta'rikh* with each one of them separately. However, as noted earlier, the copy he had, which he brought to the classes, was for the 800 fascicles arranged in 80 volumes. But these teachers did not study the expanded version with Ibn 'Asakir. They studied it with al-Qasim. With Ibn 'Asakir, they only studied the original 570 fascicles version. So essentially, they gave al-Birzali two certificates: one that goes all the way to Ibn 'Asakir, and one that goes only to al-Qasim. They also told him how al-Qasim studied it with his father so that the expanded version is "linked" back to Ibn 'Asakir. Al-Birzali wrote those certificates repeatedly on his own volumes of the *Ta'rikh*. But al-Birzali was not always systematic in writing down the information about his transmission from these teachers or about where the fascicles end and which version he followed. Sometimes he gave the date for when he copied a given fascicle of the *Ta'rikh* and another time he specified the date for when he studied it with one or more of these teachers. Similarly, he sometimes specified on his own copy where the end of a fascicle from the 570 version occurred in relation to the 800 version, but often he just gave a number without specifying if it was for the original or expanded version.

This has confused modern scholars who edited the *Ta'rikh*. They mistook what al-Birzali did, and thought the two versions overlapped, and that the notes of al-Birzali recorded the history of each manuscript, which is not the case. As said above, he identified how his teachers got their certificates from Ibn 'Asakir for the 570 fascicles and from al-Qasim for the 800 fascicles, how al-Qasim got his from his father, and then how al-Birzali himself got his certificate from them. As far as we can tell, very few extant manuscripts were squarely based on the original version. Most of them reproduce the expanded version, and might indicate in the text where it corresponds in relation to the original.

Transmission

The *Ta'rikh* was first introduced on Tuesday, 16 Rabi' I 559/12 February 1164. Ibn 'Asakir held a teaching session at the Umayyad Mosque and it took two days to finish fascicle one. The reader, who read most of the first ten fascicles, except for a few instances when Ibn 'Asakir himself did some parts, was a local scholar and notable merchant called 'Umar b. Muhammad al-'Ulaymi (d. 574/1179). The first ten fascicles took five weeks to finish, from 16 Rabi' I 559/12 February 1164 until 23 Rabi' II 559/20 March 1164.

Al-Qasim was not present for those meetings, even though his son Muhammad was there, which begs the question: why was he absent? He only appears during the re-teaching of these fascicles, which occurred between early Muharram and early Safar 560/mid-November to late December 1164, and where he was the reader. The answer must have been, as mentioned above, the tension between Ibn 'Asakir and al-Qasim over the transcription of the *Ta'rikh* from the rough copy, and that Ibn 'Asakir wanted to teach his son a lesson for not giving it his best, and thus banned him from joining the teaching of the *Ta'rikh*, as al-Dhahabi later commented. This must have troubled al-Qasim enormously, for it is reported that he finally came to the Umayyad Mosque, where his father was teaching the *Ta'rikh*, to apologize, and the two reconciled.

From the transmission notes on the different manuscripts, it can be said that shortly after al-Qasim finished the transcription of a fascicle, Ibn 'Asakir held a session at the Umayyad Mosque where he taught it. Indeed, al-Qasim wrote in the transmission note of fascicle 530 that he finished transcribing it in the last ten days of Rabi' I 565/mid-December 1169. We also read in the same note that he was the reader for the session held to teach fascicle 530, which occurred on 5 Rabi' II 565/27 December 1169 in the Umayyad Mosque. The transmission of the original copy of the *Ta'rikh* must have been completed before the end of 565/Summer of 1170.

Therefore, it can be asserted that Ibn 'Asakir circulated the original version of 570 fascicles himself. Then, he and al-Qasim embarked on some revisions, which produced the 800 fascicles. By the time it was ready, Ibn 'Asakir was too old to circulate it. It was al-Qasim who started teaching the expanded version of the *Ta'rikh*; first in the College of Hadith on 2 Sha'ban 571/15 February 1176, twenty-two days after Ibn 'Asakir had died. He finished on Friday, 28 Sha'ban 577/6 January 1182. Al-Qasim also taught the text on several other occasions and in different locations. For instance, we know that he finished another teaching in Damascus in Rabi' I 582/September 1186, and also transmitted parts of the text to a group of people outside Acre in Jumada 586/October 1190, and then back in Damascus for a few years starting in Dhu al-Hijja 587/December 1191 and again in 595/1198–596/1199.

Manuscripts

We know from many sources that the *Ta'rikh* circulated everywhere in the Muslim world. Manuscripts of it are found in every major classical library, whether in Damascus, Cairo, Istanbul, and even Patna (India). Nevertheless, there is no complete copy of the *Ta'rikh* extant, which has complicated the process of editing it. Five nearly complete sets exist:

1. Zahiriyya A: An early-eighteenth-century manuscript, which was originally owned by the famous governor of Damascus Sulayman Pasha al-'Azm (d. 1156/1743). It was later acquired by the Zahiriyya Library (the entire Zahiriyya collection was moved to the Asad Library sometime in the late 1980s). It comprises nineteen volumes, written beginning in 1118/1706 and by different hands. It must have been based on al-Birzali's personal copy.

2. Zahiriyya B: This manuscript set also dates from around 1118/1706 and was later purchased by As'ad Pasha al-'Azm (d. 1171/1758) in the year 1161/1748. It comprises nine large volumes; it is only missing the introductory volume. It was likely copied from the same original text as Zahiriyya A.

3. Ahmad III: A nearly complete sixteenth-century copy of the Ta'rikh, this manuscript at the Topkapi Library in Istanbul contains twelve large volumes. It once belonged to Sultan Ahmad III (r. 1115/1703–1143/1730).

4. Ibn Yusuf: An early eighteenth-century copy at the Ibn Yusuf Library in Marrakesh, Morocco. It originally comprised thirty-one volumes, only twenty-seven exist, and they roughly cover the beginning to the end, with some lacunae.

5. Azhar: The fifteen volumes at the al-Azhar Library in Cairo actually came from several incomplete sets of the Ta'rikh. Some of the volumes seem to be the oldest extant ones and were written by al-Birzali between 609/1213 and 619/1222; it is very likely that this copy by al-Birzali was split at one point and the first volumes of it ended up at the Khuda Bakhsh Oriental Public Library in Patna, India.

Moreover, individual volumes or small sets of volumes are dispersed in public and university libraries all over the world, such as at Dar al-Kutub in Cairo, Cambridge University, Yale University, Bibliothèque

Nationale in Paris, the British Museum, al-Zaytuna in Tunisia, and many others.

Impact

It is not an exaggeration to say that Ibn 'Asakir's *Ta'rikh* was one of the most heavily used sources from the time it first circulated until the present. Scholars realized its unique qualities and massive breadth, and used it as an essential sourcebook for Hadith as well as historical anecdotes and biographical information, especially on Damascus and Damascenes up to Ibn 'Asakir's time. For instance, one rarely comes across a biography of a Damascene scholar in al-Dhahabi's *Ta'rikh al-islam* and *Siyar a'lam al-nubala'* where Ibn 'Asakir is not quoted. The same applies to *Tahdhib al-Kamal fi asma' al-rijal* (*Perfecting the Perfect on Hadith Transmitters*) of Jamal al-Din al-Mizzi (d. 742/1341), and *Tabaqat al-shafi'iyya* (*The Great Generations of Shafi'i Scholars*) of al-Subki (d. 771/1370), where we find entire biographies or sections copied verbatim from Ibn 'Asakir's *Ta'rikh*.

The *Ta'rikh* also inspired other scholars to follow its lead, such as Ibn al-'Adim (d. 660/1262) who produced a similar work on Aleppo entitled *Bughyat al-talab fi ta'rikh Halab* (*The Pursued Desire on the History of Aleppo*). Moreover, the massive size of the *Ta'rikh* encouraged scholars to make it more accessible by abridging it or extracting selections from it. This actually started shortly after Ibn 'Asakir's death, for his son al-Qasim produced the first selection from the *Ta'rikh*, which he taught in 591/1195 and it is still extant. Subsequently, very prominent scholars in Syria and Egypt made their own selections from the *Ta'rikh*, such as *Fakihat al-majalis wa-fukahat al-mujalis* (*Fruits for Gatherings and Humor for Companions*) by Ibn 'Abd al-Da'im (d. 668/1270), a renowned scribe who was reputed to have copied the entire *Ta'rikh* twice. Another famous abridgment, entitled *al-Muntaqa min Ta'rikh Ibn 'Asakir* (*Selections from the History of Ibn 'Asakir*), was made by the notable Shafi'i jurist Ibn Qadi Shuhba (d. 851/1448), whose mother was from the 'Asakir family and who also made an abridgment of the first volume, which is dedicated to the city of Damascus. Other abridgments include *Ta'liq min Ta'rikh Ibn 'Asakir* (*Selected Assortment with Comments from the History of Ibn 'Asakir*) by the celebrated scholar of Hadith Ibn Hajar al-'Asqalani (d. 852/1449), and *Tuhfat al-mudhakir al-muntaqa min Ta'rikh Ibn 'Asakir (Gems for the Learner, being Selections from the History of Ibn 'Asakir*) by the illustrious al-Suyuti (d. 911/1505), among others.

The two most important abridgments (sing., *Mukhtasar*) of the *Ta'rikh* were those made by fellow Damascene historian Abu Shama (d. 665/1268) and by the Cairene lexicographer Ibn Manzur (d. 711/1311). Abu Shama's abridgment is in fifteen volumes; he also produced even a shorter abridgment in five volumes. Ibn Manzur's abridgment, which became the most popular of all abridgments, is in twenty-nine volumes. Ibn Manzur also made a continuation of the *Ta'rikh* — entitled *Takmilat Ta'rikh Dimashq* — in six volumes. There was a third abridgment made by al-Dhahabi in ten volumes, but it did not survive, and a fourth abridgment, entitled *al-'Aqd al-manzum al-fakhir bi-talkhis Ta'rikh Ibn 'Asakir (The Finely Adorned Neckless, being the Abridgment of the History of Ibn 'Asakir*), was made by the Hadith scholar Isma'il al-'Ajluni (d. 1162/1749).

As for continuations (sing., *Dhayl*) of the *Ta'rikh*, we can be certain of only two: that prepared by al-Qasim, but it seems he did not complete it, and that done by Ibn Manzur as noted above. It is alleged that other historians authored continuations of the *Ta'rikh* but this is incorrect and many scholars who repeated this did not bother to verify the claims, which were part of the growing legacy of Ibn 'Asakir and the eagerness of some to augment his impact on scholarly life. For instance, it is said that 'Alam al-Din al-Qasim b. Muhammad al-Birzali (d. 739/1339), who was the great grandson of al-Birzali mentioned above, wrote a continuation of the *Ta'rikh*, but this is incorrect. *Al-Muqtafi 'ala Dhayl al-Rawdatayn (The Sequel of the Continuation of the Two Gardens)* by 'Alam al-Din al-Birzali — who interestingly held the professorship of Hadith at the College of Hadith in Damascus, the post originally created for Ibn 'Asakir, as mentioned in Chapter 2 — was a continuation of Abu Shama's *Dhayl 'ala al-Rawdatayn (Continuation of the Two Gardens)*, which in turn was a continuation of his own *al-Rawdatayn fi akhbar al-dawlatayn al-nuriyya wa-l-salahiyya (The Two Gardens Concerning the Kingdoms of Nur al-Din and Saladin)*. Both 'Alam al-Din's *al-Muqtafi* and Abu Shama's *Dhayl* share nothing with Ibn 'Asakir's *Ta'rikh*, although one might say the authors were inspired by it and were eager to continue the tradition he had started (for more on this, see Chapter 6). They arranged their material in chronological order by year: first for events, followed by those who died in that year.

To return to the impact of the *Ta'rikh*, many incorporated it into their own works. One notable case is 'Izz al-Din Ibn Shaddad (d. 684/1285) in his *al-A'laq al-khatira fi dhikr al-Sham wa-l-Jazira* (*The Noteworthy Treasures on Syria and Upper Mesopotamia*). The *A'laq* is a historical-geographical source for Syria and Upper Mesopotamia (*al-Jazira*) covering the period from the beginning of times and until 659/1261, and it features massive parts lifted entirely from Ibn 'Asakir's *Ta'rikh*. Similarly, al-Mizzi, al-Subki, and al-Dhahabi did the same, as mentioned earlier, and also the anthologist al-Badri (d. 894/1489) who used heavily the parts of the *Ta'rikh* that describe the city of Damascus in his *Nuzhat al-anam fi mahasin al-Sham* (*A Picnic into the Beauties of Damascus*), which he wrote while in Cairo.

All of this demonstrates how important Ibn 'Asakir's *Ta'rikh* was in the scholarly life in Syria and beyond. Therefore, to fully grasp and measure its impact, one cannot only look at the number of its manuscripts and their circulation. We must also take into account all of the abridgments and selections as additional proof of its continued relevance and influence, and by extension the continued legacy of Ibn 'Asakir. Moreover, realizing that those who made the abridgments and selections were among the most influential professors in Syria and Egypt in their days, one can easily see that their efforts were not only to make the book accessible to scholars like themselves, but more importantly to their students. This illustrates for us another significant impact for Ibn 'Asakir's *Ta'rikh* — its enduring influence on the educational system in the pre-modern Islamic college (*madrasa*) — a subject we will return to in Chapter 6.

Modern Editions

Since the beginning of the twentieth century, Ibn 'Asakir's *Ta'rikh* has received tremendous attention due to its relevance to the projects of creating both a modern Syrian national identity and an Arab national identity, as we will see in Chapter 7. The course of its publication, however, was tortuous due to its massive size. The Hanbali scholar 'Abd al-Qadir Badran (d. 1346/1927) made an abridged edition – entitled *Tahdhib Ta'rikh Dimashq al-kabir* (*Abridgment of the Great History of Damascus*) – in thirteen volumes, but only five were published between 1911 and 1914 by Matba'at Rawdat al-Sham (lit., the Garden of Syria Press; the "garden" being Damascus). Badran could not shepherd the remaining volumes through the press due to the gradual loss of his eyesight and deteriorating health. The unpublished volumes passed to the possession of Ahmad 'Ubayd, a local Damascene scholar, playwright, and founder of the bookstore and publishing house named al-Maktaba al-'Arabiyya (the Arabic Library). In 1930 and 1932, 'Ubayd published two more volumes.

Realizing the significance of the work, the Arab Scientific Academy of Damascus (*al-Majma' al-'Ilmi al-'Arabi bi-Dimashq*) – which in 1958 was renamed the Academy of Arabic Language of Damascus (*Majma' al-Lugha al-'Arabiyya bi-Dimashq*) – took the initiative in the late 1940s to edit the entire work anew. This, too, proved to be a lengthy and complicated endeavor. The two introductory volumes of the *Ta'rikh* were published in 1951 and 1954 by Salah al-Din al-Munajjid. The next volume to come out was volume 10 in 1964. Two subsequent volumes (nos. 31 and 37) came out in 1978 and 1979. The project really picked up steam in the mid-1980s and afterwards, largely thanks to the heroic efforts of Sukayna al-Shihabi (d. 2006), who alone edited thirty-two volumes between 1984 and 2006. (Prior to her inclusion in the project, she had published in 1982 the last two volumes of the *Ta'rikh* on women, although she did so outside this series.) To date, fifty-seven volumes out of eighty (nos. 1–4, 7, 10–12, 18–23, 25–29, 31–54, 59–71, and 76) have been published (in a haphazard order); the last volumes published were nos. 26, 28, 29, and 76, and they came out in 2020.

In 1996, Dar al-Fikr, in Beirut and Damascus, began the publication of a new edition, which was completed in 2000. Actually, this edition was begun by Dar al-Fikr in 1994 and the editor was 'Ali Shiri of Lebanon. But it was then commandeered by 'Umar al-'Amrawi of

Saudi Arabia and his name was put as the lead editor, and in subsequent reprints Dar al-Fikr removed the name of Shiri entirely. It could be that this happened because Shiri is a Shi'i, posing a problem for marketing the book to Salafis and Sunni Islamists especially in Saudi Arabia, and also partly because al-'Amrawi (who otherwise has no expertise in Islamic history) contributed to underwriting the cost of publication. The Dar al-Fikr edition comprises eighty volumes (seventy for the *Ta'rikh*, four for addenda and lacunae that are not in any of the manuscripts but were taken from medieval abridgments of it or other sources that quoted Ibn 'Asakir, and six for indices). The quality of this edition is inferior, and it contains countless errors and typos due to the rush to finish it.

Another complete edition was made by 'Ali 'Ashur and published in Beirut in 2001 by Dar Ihya' al-Turath al-'Arabi. It comprises thirty-nine volumes. Aside from these, several individual biographies from the *Ta'rikh* have been published separately by different scholars.

THE 'ASAKIR EXTENDED FAMILY

Several members of the 'Asakir family distinguished themselves in the scholarly and administrative life of medieval Syria. Some of them were direct descendants of Ibn 'Asakir, while the majority were descendants of his younger brother Muhammad. All of them were involved in one way or another in Hadith scholarship between the sixth/twelfth and eighth/fourteenth centuries, and some were luminaries in the field. Some rose to prominence in social, legal, and administrative professions as well. That we cannot trace the family after the eighth/fourteenth century (except for two cases: see the family tree at the end of Chapter 5) could likely be the result of its members dropping the use of the "Ibn 'Asakir" surname. It could also be that they were attracted to other professions than Hadith and religious scholarship.

There is one interesting observation about their honorifics – *Abu X* or *Umm X*. Each member of the family was given his/her honorific at the time of birth, which does not necessarily indicate that the person in question had a son by that name. In theory, an honorific in the Arab social custom follows the name of the first son, irrespective of whether or not he lived or died in childhood, and also irrespective of whether or not he is preceded by sisters. But with the members of the 'Asakir family this did not seem to be the case, indicating a change that started to take place around that time in the Muslim world. For instance, Ibn 'Asakir's father had the honorific Abu Muhammad, and we know that his last son was named Muhammad. Similarly, the honorific of Ibn 'Asakir's mother was Umm al-Qasim, even though she did not have a son by that name. Ibn 'Asakir himself was given the

honorific Abu al-Qasim when he was born. It is said that Abu al-Qasim 'Ali b. Ibrahim al-Husayni – the well-known Damascene scholar
and later teacher of Ibn 'Asakir – asked Ibn 'Asakir's father al-Hasan
what name he gave to his newborn son, and al-Hasan replied: "I called
him Abu al-Qasim 'Ali," to which the scholar wittily responded: "You
called him then after me."

That Ibn 'Asakir later on called his firstborn son al-Qasim does not
undermine this remark. As with the case of Ibn 'Asakir's parents, most
of his nephews and later members of the family did not have sons who
matched their honorifics, and some had sons by those names but who
were not their firstborn. For instance, his notable nephew al-Hasan
had the honorific Abu al-Barakat, but no son by that name. Nor did
his other notable nephew 'Abd al-Rahman, whose honorific was Abu
Mansur, have a son by that name.

I list and identify below the most important members of the 'Asakir
family: his direct descendants as well as the descendants of his sister
whose name we do not know, his brother Muhammad, and his uncle
al-Muzaffar. The purpose of doing this is not merely to highlight their
own individual accomplishments. It is rather intended to demonstrate
how Ibn 'Asakir's legacy lived on through the members of his family,
and how they enriched it and augmented it. Many of them played an
active role in the teaching and dissemination of Ibn 'Asakir's works.
More importantly they, explicitly or implicitly, kept his memory alive
and "reminded" those they taught and interacted with of their towering ancestor. The scholars who studied with Ibn 'Asakir's immediate
descendants and subsequent generations of the 'Asakir family became
some of the most authoritative and reputable authorities of Hadith
and Sunni jurisprudence in Damascus, Syria, Egypt, and elsewhere.
This vividly illustrates Ibn 'Asakir's enduring impact not only in terms
of the books he wrote or the advocacy he engaged in on behalf of
the revivification and empowerment of Sunnism, but also his role in
launching a family of remarkable scholars, each of whom made their
own individual imprint on this Sunni renaissance. The fact that members of the 'Asakir family sustained this significant role for several generations over at least three centuries, especially in Damascus, only
cemented the family's notoriety. In fact, one could plausibly argue

that, between the sixth/twelfth and eighth/fourteenth centuries, it was nearly impossible for any Damascene student to pursue the serious study of Hadith and not study at the feet of a member of the 'Asakir family at some point.

DIRECT DESCENDANTS OF IBN 'ASAKIR

Ibn 'Asakir married his maternal cousin 'A'isha bt. 'Ali al-Sulami (d. 564/1169) and they had at least three children. The firstborn was Abu Muhammad al-Qasim (527/1133–600/1203), who followed his father's example and became an acclaimed Hadith scholar and inherited the chair of Hadith at the College of Hadith in Damascus. His most significant contribution was the transcription of the massive Ta'rikh from the loose notes and rough draft of his father into proper volumes, and then finishing the expanded version and teaching it to students, thus assuring its survival and dissemination, as well as so many other works by his father. He also composed a continuation of the Ta'rikh, and authored a significant treatise on the merits of Jerusalem entitled al-Mustaqsa fi fada'il al-masjid al-aqsa (The Exhaustive Treatise on the Merits of the Aqsa Sanctuary), which became the main source for many later works on the religious merits of Jerusalem during the Mamluk period, such as Ba'ith al-nufus ila ziyarat al-Quds al-mahrus (Revival of the Spirits on the Pilgrimage to Jerusalem) by Ibn al-Firkah (d. 729/1329). Al-Qasim also wrote Kitab al-Jihad (Book on Jihad), which he taught to Saladin in 579/1183. Indeed, he wrote that at the beginning and the conclusion of that class, he invoked God to facilitate Saladin's conquest of Jerusalem, and that God had answered his prayer (al-Dhahabi, Siyar 21: 411). That he was there to witness Saladin's capture of the city in Rajab 583/October 1187 suggests his close relationship to the Ayyubid Sultan. Neither book – al-Mustaqsa or Kitab al-Jihad – appears to have survived (the alleged manuscripts of the former and an edition are actually of a much later work on the religious merits of Jerusalem that plagiarized al-Qasim's book). Al-Qasim also abridged his father's Ta'rikh, an extant copy of which is still in the Zahiriyya collection in Damascus.

Ibn 'Asakir had a daughter named Halima. Nothing other than her name is known about her. He also had another son named Abu al-Fath al-Hasan (d. 600/1204), who did not seem to have developed any serious expertise. Al-Hasan's two sons, 'Abd Allah and Muhammad as well as his grandson 'Umar were minor Hadith scholars.

Al-Qasim had three sons. The firstborn was named Abu Tahir Muhammad, born before 653/1167. We encounter his name in some teaching sessions of Ibn 'Asakir's books, but nothing else is known about him. The second son was called Abu al-Qasim 'Ali (581/1185–616/1219) after his grandfather. He became a Hadith scholar and occupied the chair of Hadith at the College of Hadith following his father. During that time, he travelled to Khurasan seeking further Hadith education, although very likely he was after specific certificates and precious short chains of transmission, since we know that he taught Hadith on his way there, such as in Irbil in Rajab 614/October 1217. It is said that he was the last Damascene to have made such a trip, as the Mongol attacks meant Syrians stopped travelling to the east for religious education. He died in Baghdad on his return journey from fatal wounds inflicted by robbers who attacked him. It is also said that he held Shi'i sympathies to the dismay of his family and the Damascene Sunni establishment. Al-Qasim had another son called 'Abd al-Rahman, about whom nothing else is known.

Some of Ibn 'Asakir's great grandchildren rose to prominence. Among them, two are worth noting. His great granddaughter Fatima bt. 'Ali, nicknamed *Umm al-'Arab* (Mother of the Arabs), was a prominent Hadith scholar. Born in 598/1202, she started her education in Damascus at the age of five, and her family's contacts assured her a large number of certificates from prestigious scholars across the Muslim world. Her Hadith scholarship was sought after for the quality of her chains of transmission, which ironically bypassed her famed great-grandfather, on account of the fact that the best chains of transmission were those that provided the fewest number of informants that could be reliably traced back to the Prophet Muhammad. She married her second cousin 'Abd al-Latif b. al-Hasan b. Muhammad (b. 600/1204), who at one point was a companion of the celebrated Sufi mystic Abu Hafs al-Suhrawardi (d. 632/1234) in Baghdad. Their son

'Abd al-Mun'im (625/1228–700/1301) was also a prominent Hadith scholar and a Sufi. She died in 683/1284.

The last person we know of Ibn 'Asakir's direct lineage is Taj al-Din 'Abd al-Wahhab b. Muhammad who was a classmate of al-Dhahabi and died relatively young in 691/1292. His father Badr al-Din Muhammad b. al-Husayn (d. 712/1313) was a certified notary in Damascus and then secretary for various governors in different places, including Yemen. Muhammad had three sons; but we only know the name of 'Abd al-Wahhab.

DESCENDANTS OF IBN 'ASAKIR'S SISTER

Ibn 'Asakir had a sister, but we do not know her name. She was married to Abu Bakr Muhammad b. 'Ali al-Sulami (d. 564/1169) from the notable Sulami family of Damascus. He was the son of Abu al-Hasan al-Sulami mentioned several times before. Abu Bakr al-Sulami became the chief orator of the Umayyad Mosque and inherited the professorship of Shafi'i law at the Aminiyya College after his father. Their son Abu al-Hasan 'Ali (544/1149–602/1206) was a notable scholar and professor of law at the Aminiyya College, a post that his father and grandfather had occupied, but toward the end of his life he fell out of favor with the Ayyubid rulers of the city and was expelled from Damascus. He died in Hims.

DESCENDANTS OF IBN 'ASAKIR'S BROTHER MUHAMMAD

It was the descendants of Ibn 'Asakir's younger brother Muhammad who continued the family's legacy and occupied a prestigious place in Damascene society for centuries to come, most notably his grandson Muhammad (565/1170–643/1245), who was nicknamed *al-Sadr* for his preeminence as one of the social elites in the city. It should be noted that Muhammad's wife, Asma' bt. Muhammad al-Bazzaz (d. 594/1198), who was also his maternal cousin, was an accomplished Hadith scholar in her own right. Hence, one expects she had a hand in her children's education and their rising to prominence as well. The most prominent descendants of Muhammad who were distinguished for their scholarly contribution are listed below.

Abu al-Fadl Ahmad b. Muhammad (542/1147–610/1213)
A scholar of Hadith, he also held several administrative positions in Damascus including the post of judge in the city. He was known to have transmitted *Kitab al-Sunan* of al-Daraqutni, which he studied with his uncle Hibat Allah. He was nicknamed *Taj al-Umana'*, meaning the crown of the trusted ones. He wrote a book on the merits of Jerusalem, entitled *al-Uns fi fada'il al-quds (Familiarizing Oneself with the Merits of Jerusalem)*, which he finished in Shawwal 603/May 1207.

Abu al-Barakat al-Hasan b. Muhammad (544/1149–627/1230)
A notable scholar of Hadith and senior official in the Ayyubid administration, he occupied several prestigious posts, including that of Inspector of the Treasury in Damascus. He also inherited the family chair at the College of Hadith after the death of 'Ali b. al-Qasim, the grandson of Ibn 'Asakir. His nickname was *Zayn al-Umana'*, meaning the most magnificent of the trusted ones. His role in the preservation and dissemination of Ibn 'Asakir's works was immense.

Abu al-Muzaffar 'Abd Allah b. Muhammad (549/1154–591/1195)
He was a professor at the Taqawiyya College of Hadith in Damascus, having studied (obviously beside his famous uncle) with Damascus' chief-judge Qutb al-Din al-Naysaburi and others as well. He was killed by robbers outside Cairo.

Abu Mansur 'Abd al-Rahman b. Muhammad (550/1155–620/1223)
Nicknamed *Fakhr al-Din* (the pride of religion), he was a renowned scholar of Hadith and jurisprudence, and later became the mufti* of Damascus. He married the daughter of Qutb al-Din al-Naysaburi and followed him as leader of the Shafi'is in Syria. He also occupied several prestigious chairs for the study of Hadith and jurisprudence, including the Salihiyya College in Jerusalem and the Taqawiyya College in Damascus after his brother 'Abd Allah. When his grand-nephew (Ibn 'Asakir's grandson 'Ali) was away, he filled in as chair of Hadith

at the College of Hadith. He was offered the post of chief-judge of Damascus after the death of his mentor and father-in-law, but turned it down. Among his notable students was the celebrated al-'Izz Ibn 'Abd al-Salam. He left a few works, one of which is entitled *al-Arba'un fi manaqib ummahat al-mu'minin* (*Forty Hadiths on the Virtues of the Widows of Muhammad*), which is extant. His role in the preservation and dissemination of Ibn 'Asakir's works was immense.

Abu al-Hasan 'Abd al-Wahhab b. al-Hasan b. Muhammad (591/1195–660/1262)

He was an authority on Hadith and assumed the chair at the College of Hadith after his father al-Hasan b. Muhammad. He was nicknamed *Taj al-Din* (crown of religion). He died in Mecca while on a retreat there.

Asma' bt. al-Hasan b. Muhammad (d. 680/1282)

She was a Hadith scholar and received many certificates and taught extensively in Damascus. She married her second cousin al-Husayn b. 'Ali (Ibn 'Asakir's great-grandson).

Abu al-Yumn 'Abd al-Samad b. 'Abd al-Wahhab (614/1217–686/1287)

Known as *Amin al-Din* (the trustee of religion), he followed in his father's footsteps and became a leading scholar of Hadith. He then moved to Mecca and became a leading scholar of Hadith in the Hijaz and authored a few works of his own, including a short treatise entitled *Fi na'l al-nabi* (*On the Sandal of the Prophet Muhammad*), which is extant. He was also known for his quasi-ascetic lifestyle. He died in Medina.

Amina bt. 'Abd al-Rahim b. Muhammad (d. 689/1290)

She was an eminent Hadith scholar who was nicknamed *Sitt al-Umana'* (the lady of the trusted ones). Among her students were two of the most famous luminaries of the eighth/fourteenth century: 'Alam al-Din al-Birzali and al-Mizzi.

Abu al-Fadl Ahmad b. Hibat Allah b. Ahmad (614/1217–699/1300)

Nicknamed *Sharaf al-Din* (the eminence of religion), he was one of the most renowned Hadith scholars of his age in Damascus. He was the grandson of Abu al-Fadl Ahmad, and was known for teaching the *Sahih* of al-Bukhari, *Sahih* of Muslim, *Muwatta'* of Malik, as well as many other Hadith books and also the *Tafsir* of al-Baghawi (d. 516/1122) and the *Risala* of al-Qushayri (d. 465/1072). Among his teachers was the famous historian Ibn al-Athir (d. 630/1233). He taught the likes of 'Alam al-Din al-Birzali, al-Mizzi, and al-Dhahabi.

Abu Muhammad al-Qasim b. al-Muzaffar (629/1231–723/1323)
The great-grandson of Ahmad b. Muhammad, he was a great authority of Hadith and well-known physician who treated his patients free of charge. He also occupied a senior post in the office of the Treasury in Damascus. He was the teacher of 'Alam al-Din al-Birzali and al-Dhahabi.

OTHER MEMBERS OF THE 'ASAKIR FAMILY

Ibn 'Asakir had an uncle called al-Muzaffar. Nothing else is known about him. His grandson Abu Tahir Mu'ayyad al-Din Isma'il b. 'Uthman became the secretary and then vizier for the governor of Qus (in Upper Egypt) Badr al-Din al-Hakkari, who assumed his post around 586/1190, toward the end of Saladin's reign. Isma'il was also a poet.

Isma'il's son Majd al-Din Abu 'Abd Allah Muhammad b. Isma'il (587/1191–669/1271) grew up and studied primarily in Damascus and was well known in the Hadith circles of Ayyubid and early Mamluk Syria and Egypt. He was an authority on *Kitab al-Tajrid* of Ibn al-Fahham al-Siqilli (d. 516/1122), which addresses the seven canonical readings (*qira'at*) of the Qur'an.

Muhammad's son Mu'ayyad al-Din Abu al-'Abbas Ahmad (611/1214–676/1278) was also a famous Hadith scholar and left a legacy of his own in Egypt. Ahmad's great grandson, Muhammad b. al-Hasan b. 'Abd al-Wahid b. Ahmad (d. 952/1545), was the imam of a local mosque in Damascus and bequeathed his properties as well as his entire library to the mosque after his death. He is the last member of the 'Asakir family that we can identify. Most probably, the members of the family simply dropped the use of 'Asakir after him.

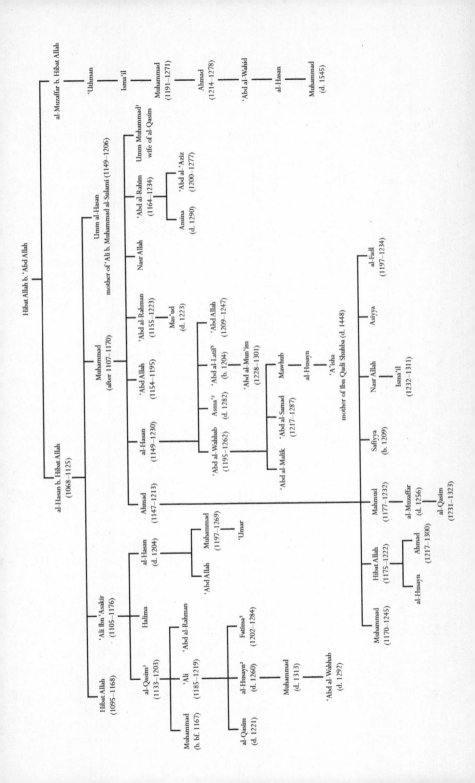

6

MEDIEVAL LEGACY

Writing in Cairo, the famous Mamluk scholar Shams al-Din al-Sakhawi (d. 902/1497) penned in his *al-I'lan bi-l-tawbikh li-man dhamm al-tarikh* (*A Rebuke to the Disparager of History*) that religious knowledge weakened in Damascus during the fourth/tenth and fifth/eleventh centuries. He added that it resurged under Sultan Nur al-Din, thanks to the city's celebrated Hadith scholar Ibn 'Asakir and the Jerusalemites (al-Sakhawi, *al-I'lan* 294). The Jerusalemites were actually a family of Hanbali scholars from the town of Jamma'il, near Nablus (north of Jerusalem) who eventually refused to live under Crusader rule. They moved to Damascus in 551/1156 and inhabited the al-Salihiyya neighborhood (located on the eastern slope of Mount Qasyun, northwest of the city). They were some of the most active scholars in Syria during the late sixth/twelfth and seventh/thirteenth centuries. Among them was one of the most celebrated Hanbali scholars of all time, Ibn Qudama (d. 620/1223). Nevertheless, that Ibn 'Asakir was the only scholar al-Sakhawi identified by name is a testimony to his towering legacy in Sunnism.

Indeed, it is almost impossible to come across a scholar commenting on the history of Damascus and the revivification of Sunnism there and in Syria who does not mention the key role played by Ibn 'Asakir. It is also almost impossible to come across a biographical dictionary written after him that does not give a nod to Ibn 'Asakir. I have already discussed (in Chapter 2) anecdotes that speak of the dreams that Ibn 'Asakir's parents had, where each one heard a voice proclaiming the birth of a boy who will revivify Sunnism. These two are repeated here:

I [al-Qasim] used to hear my father [Ibn 'Asakir] say that, while his
mother was pregnant, his father had a vision in a dream informing him
that he would beget a son whom God would use to revivify Sunnism.

(Yaqut al-Hamawi, Mu'jam al-udaba' 4: 1702)

When my mother became pregnant with me, she saw in her dream
someone telling her: "You will beget a child who will become very
important. When you deliver him, bring him on the fortieth day of his
birth to the Grotto – meaning the Grotto of Blood in Mount Qasyun
– and give alms, for then God will bless him and bless the Muslims by
him."

(al-Subki, Tabaqat al-shafi'iyya 4: 139)

The famous eighth-/fourteenth-century scholar Ibn Kathir (d.
774/1373) reproduced these two reports in his biography of Ibn
'Asakir, and then interjected the following comment:

I say that these visions are indeed true, and what proves it is that he
brought to Syria the most famous books of Islam, such as the Musnad
of Ahmad [Ibn Hanbal], the Musnad of Abu Ya'la al-Mawsili, and other
Hadith books, the massive ones and concise ones.

(Ibn Kathir, Tabaqat al-fuqaha' al-shafi'iyyin 1: 694)

The words of Ibn Kathir underline the esteem with which subsequent
Sunni scholars evaluated Ibn 'Asakir's substantial contribution to the
Sunni revival in Syria. His seminal role in the introduction of some of
the weightiest books of the canon of Sunnism paved the way for this
revival. Without them, the revival would not have taken place.

Taj al-Din al-Subki (d. 771/1370), one of Damascus's celebrated
scholars, went even further in his accolade of Ibn 'Asakir:

He is the leading teacher, the protector of the Sunna and its servant,
the vanquisher of Satan's army by his scholarship and their slayer, the
leader of Hadith scholars in his day, and the last of the great memorizers
of Hadith. No one can deny his eminence, for it is the desire of those
who embark on the journey of knowledge and the endpoint for those
who have great resolve among the seekers. He is the sine qua non by
the unanimous agreement of the community, the attainer of what is
beyond aspirations, the ocean that is not bounded by a shoreline, and
the erudite who carried the burden of spreading the Sunna. He spent his

days and nights indefatigably pursuing all fields of scholarship. His only companions were knowledge and hard work, for they were his utmost desire. His memory captured even the slightest detail, his precision combined the new and the old, his command put him on par with those who came before him if not exceeding them, and his breadth of knowledge was so enriching that everyone else was as a beggar compared to him.

(Al-Subki, *Tabaqat al-shafi'iyya* 4: 137)

These words of al-Subki are a bit over the top. No doubt, one should take them with a grain of salt, for hyperbole was a literary style. Nevertheless, this is not the typical language that al-Subki employed in his biographies of other figures in his dictionary of Shafi'i scholars. That he and so many like him went out of their way in their praise of Ibn 'Asakir reflects their realization that their distinguished forerunner stood head and shoulders above his peers. For them, Ibn 'Asakir's exceptional knowledge of and the unique role he played in the dissemination of Hadith scholarship assured him a special status in Sunni scholarly genealogy.

One can even say that Ibn 'Asakir's promotion of Hadith as the cornerstone of Islamic religious knowledge, and his role in disseminating the canonical books of Hadith ensured that later generations who followed his path would see him as an exemplary and pioneering figure. After all, since the study of Hadith was so central to their intellectual formation, they could not help but see Ibn 'Asakir as a model and a pioneer for them to emulate.

Nevertheless, despite all the accolades, there were occasional criticisms of Ibn 'Asakir levelled by some of those who admired him the most. Al-Dhahabi, for instance, was effusive in his praise for Ibn 'Asakir:

There was no one in his time equal to him in the command of Hadith or more knowledgeable about Hadith transmitters. Whoever reads his *Ta'rikh* realizes the man's preeminence.

(al-Dhahabi, *Ta'rikh* 40: 72)

Yet, al-Dhahabi criticized Ibn 'Asakir for reproducing in his many works questionable hadiths. Ibn 'Asakir did indeed transmit many hadiths known to be either weak or outright fabrications, and he had his reasons for doing so (as discussed in Chapter 4). However, those reasons did not exonerate him before some later scholars like al-Dhahabi, who said:

> Despite his eminence and great memorization of Hadith, he still chose to diffuse weak and fabricated hadiths without verifying them. This was the practice of most great memorizers after the first centuries, except for a few, and God will ask them about that. For what is the purpose of learning about the transmitters of Hadith, accounts of history and books that assess the trustworthiness of Hadith transmitters except to expose fake hadiths and rip them apart.

> (al-Dhahabi, *Ta'rikh* 40: 82)

One can clearly sense al-Dhahabi's sarcasm here: Ibn 'Asakir, because of his exceptional command of Hadith and its sciences, should have refused to traffic in fake and questionable hadiths.

Nevertheless, such criticism remained limited, and did not impact Ibn 'Asakir's towering stature among later generations, especially those who did not have a theological "grievance" against him, like some Hanbalis (as we have seen in Chapters 2 and 3).

Even some of the Hanbalis gradually warmed to him, although posthumously. Ibn Taymiyya, for instance, praised Ibn 'Asakir for his fundamental contribution to the preservation of the Islamic past. He especially applauded Ibn 'Asakir's *Tabyin* as the best book ever written on Abu al-Hasan al-Ash'ari and for its advocacy of Muslim unity. In Ibn Taymiyya's words, Ibn 'Asakir argued that the Hanbalis and Ash'aris were in accord until the major controversy unfolded in Baghdad in Shawwal 469/May 1077 between the two groups, and spread everywhere in the Muslim world. Needless to say, Ibn 'Asakir argued that it was the Hanbalis who had erred by straying from the teachings of Ahmad Ibn Hanbal, whereas Ibn Taymiyya took the view that it was the Ash'aris who had distanced themselves from the teachings of the Qur'an and the Prophet regarding the matters over which the two groups disagreed. At any rate, Ibn Taymiyya applauded Ibn 'Asakir for pointing out and promoting the unity of Sunnis (irrespective of whether or not this is historically true), and lamenting the fact that it became elusive after the famous controversy.

IBN 'ASAKIR'S NOTABLE STUDENTS

There is ample evidence that Ibn 'Asakir's students had an active role in spreading his legacy. First, his son al-Qasim and his nephews, especially al-Hasan and 'Abd al-Rahman, played a central part in the initial dissemination of his scholarship. One need only look at the thousands of classes they taught on the *Ta'rikh* in order to grasp the incredible effort this must have required. They were adamant about ensuring that the works of their father/uncle were taught to the largest number of scholars and students, especially in Damascus, and that he occupy his place of honor in the history of the city and Islam.

There were other celebrated students of Ibn 'Asakir who showed no less enthusiasm than his son and nephews. They included the brothers Abu al-Mawahib al-Hasan b. Hibat Allah Ibn Sasra (537/1142–586/1190) – whose name was originally Nasr Allah, but he changed it around 565/1170 to al-Hasan – and Abu al-Qasim al-Husayn b. Hibat Allah Ibn Sasra (before 540/1145–626/1228). Also, there were Zakiy al-Din Ibrahim b. Barakat Ibn al-Khushu'i (558/1163–640/1243), Abu Bakr Muhammad b. 'Abd al-Wahhab al-Ansari (549/1154–627/1230), and Abu Muhammad 'Abd al-'Aziz b. al-Hasan Ibn Abiyya (564/1169–640/1242). These five played a key role in the preservation and dissemination of Ibn 'Asakir's books. It is not an exaggeration to say that collectively – and in addition to Ibn 'Asakir's family – they had a role in passing down every book and seminar of their teacher. We find their names in the two types of colophons in almost every manuscript: the first type refers to colophons stating when and where they learned the book from Ibn 'Asakir, and the second type informs where and when they taught it and who studied it with them. Sometimes, we find several colophons of the second type in the same manuscript, which only shows how eager they were to teach Ibn 'Asakir's books in several locations in the city of Damascus and elsewhere in Syria and even in Egypt and the Hijaz (Mecca and Medina).

For instance, al-Hasan Ibn Sasra assisted Ibn 'Asakir in teaching the *al-Arba'un hadith fi al-hathth 'ala al-jihad* on 29 Ramadan 569/3 May 1174 in the Umayyad Mosque. Present were Ibrahim Ibn al-Khushu'i, who was then eleven years old, Muhammad al-Ansari, and 'Abd al-'Aziz Ibn Abiyya, who was five years old and came to the class in the company of his father. Ibn al-Khushu'i taught the book on his own three times after that: once on 9 Rabi' I 624/26 February 1227 in the Khatuniyya College (south-west of the Umayyad Mosque), a second time in Jumada I 626/April 1229 in the Umayyad Mosque, and a third time on 21 Shawwal 633/27 June 1236 in the Kallasa College (which was adjacent to Saladin's tomb outside the northern gate of the Umayyad Mosque complex). Similarly, Muhammad al-Ansari taught the book twice: once on 22 Rabi' I 624/12 March 1227 in the Umayyad Mosque, and a second time on 13 Safar 626/12 January 1229, also in the Umayyad Mosque. Ibn Abiyya taught the book once on 26 Rabi' I 624/16 March 1227 in the *Zawiya* of Nasr al-Maqdisi (i.e. *Zawiya* of al-Ghazali) in the Umayyad Mosque courtyard.

Equally, al-Husayn Ibn Sasra transmitted *al-Arba'un al-abdal al-'awali* (*Forty Hadiths from the First Substitutes*[*]) in Rabi' II 611/August 1214. He had studied it with Ibn 'Asakir in the Umayyad Mosque, the first time in Rabi' II 549/June–July 1154 when he was around ten years old, and a second time in Ramadan 567/May 1172. Moreover, he and his brother al-Hasan were the readers of the book *al-Arba'un hadith min al-musawat*[*] (*Forty Hadiths from al-Furawi who Related Them with the Same Number of Informants as the Authors of the Major Books of Hadith*) when Ibn 'Asakir taught it in the Umayyad Mosque in Ramadan 569/April 1174. Present were Ibn al-Khushu'i, Ibn Abiyya, and Abu Bakr 'Atiq b. Abu al-Fadl al-Salamani (553/1158–634/1237), who became a notable scholar of Hadith and a leading notary public in the city. Later on, these three jointly taught the book on 10 Sha'ban 633/19 April 1236 in Caliph 'Umar II Mosque in Damascus (located outside the eastern gate of the Umayyad Mosque complex). Abu Bakr al-Salamani was also directly involved in the transmission of Ibn 'Asakir's *Fi fadl Rajab* (*On the Virtues of the Month of Rajab*), which was Ibn 'Asakir's seminar no. 406, among other books. Also, it is said that Abu Nasr Ibn al-Shirazi (mentioned earlier in Chapter 4) transcribed and transmitted more than 200 fascicles of Ibn 'Asakir's *Ta'rikh*.

Another major figure who was not one of his students, but who played a fundamental role in the preservation and dissemination of some of Ibn 'Asakir's books, was al-Birzali (mentioned in Chapter

4). He was originally from the area of Seville (Ishbilya) in Muslim Spain, born there around 577/1181. In 610/1213, he came to settle in Damascus where he became the imam of a local mosque – known as Fulus Mosque – outside the southern Bab al-Jabiya Gate of the old city. He also occupied the professorship of Hadith at the Ibn 'Urwa College, which was located just outside the eastern gate of the Umayyad Mosque compound. It is no exaggeration to say that al-Birzali was on a crusade to copy every book by Ibn 'Asakir that he could find, and then arrange to meet the students of Ibn 'Asakir who were still alive and study these books with them. He alone is responsible for a large number of existing manuscripts of Ibn 'Asakir's books, including several volumes of the *Ta'rikh*, *Tabyin*, *al-Arba'un al-bulda-niyya* (*Forty Hadiths from Forty Notable Scholars in Forty Different Towns*), among others. We can tell which manuscripts were actually written by his own hand versus those that were later copied from his copies. The manuscripts featuring an elegant North African handwriting were by him, for he was famous for his refined penmanship. Also, the only complete manuscript of Ibn 'Asakir's *al-Arba'un hadith fi al-hathth 'ala al-jihad* was written by him on 25 Dhu al-Hijja 617/20 February 1221. Interestingly, his great-grandson 'Alam al-Din al-Birzali occupied the chair of Hadith at the College of Hadith, the school and chair that Nur al-Din had endowed for Ibn 'Asakir. 'Alam al-Din was also responsible for the transcription of some of Ibn 'Asakir's books, especially the *Ta'rikh*.

Al-Birzali arranged to have classes with several of Ibn 'Asakir's students to study the *Ta'rikh* with them (as noted in Chapter 4). With Ibn 'Asakir's nephew al-Hasan b. Muhammad, he studied the *Ta'rikh* over a period of three years (617/1220–620/1223), meeting several times a week in several places around the city (including the Umayyad Mosque and the College of Hadith) to go over the 800 fascicles of it. With Ibn 'Asakir's other nephew, 'Abd al-Rahman b. Muhammad, al-Birzali studied the *Ta'rikh* between 616/1219 and 619/1222, also a period of three years (in the Umayyad Mosque and the Jarukhiyya College). He also studied it with Abu Nasr Ibn al-Shirazi between 618/1221 and 619/1223. This shows the tremendous effort and patience it took to teach a book like the *Ta'rikh*, and the dedication of Ibn 'Asakir's students to devote a large portion of their days over a long period of time to teach it, not to mention al-Birzali's heroic effort to copy it, to study it several times, and later to teach it.

The role of Ibn 'Asakir's students in disseminating his books, and by extension his reputation, was not limited to Damascus. As we saw earlier, his son al-Qasim taught the *Ta'rikh* in Acre. Other students taught works by Ibn 'Asakir elsewhere around the Muslim world. For instance, the colophon in the edited copy of *Kashf al-mughatta,* which was the subject of twenty-three seminars (nos. 101–123) taught by Ibn 'Asakir in the College of Hadith and concluded on 28 Rajab 566/6 April 1171, featured the presence of Sharaf al-Din 'Abd al-Qadir b. Muhammad al-Baghdadi (553/1158–634/1237). Sharaf al-Din al-Baghdadi was then thirteen years old. Later on, he taught it in the Red Mosque in Cairo on 28 Dhu al-Hijja 624/9 December 1229.

Similarly, one of the surviving manuscripts of *Fi nafi al-tashbih* gives us a fascinating map on how the network of Ibn 'Asakir's students passed along his scholarship. This lone manuscript features twenty-three colophons at the end. They document teaching sessions that took place between 25 Ramadan 568/10 May 1173 and 12 Muharram 843/25 June 1439. They were held in several locations and schools in and around Damascus and Cairo, as well as in Mecca and Medina. The first teaching session, with Ibn 'Asakir no doubt, and which took place in 568/1173, featured the presence of several students, including Abu al-'Abbas Ibn Maslama (555/1160–650/1253), Abu Muhammad Ibn 'Allan (563/1168–652/1254), and Baha' al-Din Ibn al-Jummayzi, who came to Damascus in that year to specifically study the *Sahih* of al-Bukhari with Ibn 'Asakir (as mentioned in Chapter 3). The remaining twenty-two teaching sessions are traced to these three students. And note, this is the testimony of only one manuscript.

Moreover, one particular teaching session of these twenty-two shows us the kind of fame that Ibn 'Asakir had amassed in the genealogy of Sunnism. It was convened on 23 Sha'ban 732/20 May 1332 in Cairo in the home of the celebrated jurist Yahya b. Fadl Allah al-'Umari (d. 739/1339), who was also the private secretary of the Mamluk Sultan al-Nasir Muhammad (r. 693/1293–694/1294, 698/1299–708/1309, and 709/1310–741/1341) during his third turn in office.

Yahya al-'Umari had studied *Fi nafi al-tashbih* with Ibn Maslama and Ibn 'Allan. The reader was the great jurist of Shafi'i law Taqiy al-Din al-Subki (d. 744/1344), not to be confused with another person of the same nickname, of equal fame and who had a similar career, Taqiy al-Din al-Subki (d. 756/1355), originally from Damascus and the father of Taj al-Din al-Subki. Among the large crowd present were the famous jurist Ibn al-Dumyati (d. 749/1348), Taj al-Din al-Subki who idealized Ibn 'Asakir as we saw earlier and happened to be studying in Cairo that year, Taj al-Din al-Yamani (d. 743/1343), Shahab al-Din al-'Asjadi (d. 758/1357), Nur al-Din al-Isnawi (d. 775/1374), and many others.

Ibn al-Jummayzi, Ibn Maslama, and Ibn 'Allan also taught the book to countless other people, including a very active scholar named Jamal al-Din Ahmad b. Muhammad al-Zahiri (d. 696/1297) who studied it in Mecca on 5 Dhu al-Hijja 645/1 April 1248 with Ibn al-Jummayzi, and in Damascus in 651/1253 with Ibn Maslama and Ibn 'Allan. Later in his life, between 686/1287 and 690/1291, Jamal al-Din al-Zahiri – along with his son Abu Muhammad 'Uthman (d. 730/1330) – convened several sessions (eight according to this manuscript) in mosques, schools, and private residences in and around Cairo to teach Ibn 'Asakir's *Fi nafi al-tashbih* to many students, among them notable scholars, administrators, and commanders in the Mamluk administration.

The eagerness to teach and study this particular text of Ibn 'Asakir requires some explanation. The controversy over anthropomorphism between the Ash'aris and Hanbalis in Damascus and Cairo was reignited at this time. We can see its impact in the famous inquisitions of two Hanbali jurists 'Abd al-Ghani al-Maqdisi and Ibn Taymiyya, which occurred a century apart (end of the sixth/twelfth century and beginning of the eighth/fourteenth century respectively). Both scholars were tried and imprisoned for some time on account of their ardent defense of anthropomorphism. The trials were widely publicized and generated many scholarly debates, heightened attention, and even some violence, especially in Damascus (where debates started) and Cairo (where they concluded, because Cairo was the seat of the Sultan's court). Interestingly, Abu Muhammad 'Uthman, the son of Jamal al-Din al-Zahiri mentioned above, wrote a letter to one of his friends in Damascus to report on the division among the Cairene jurists over Ibn Taymiyya's trial.

Therefore, the transmission of Ibn 'Asakir's *Fi nafi al-tashbih* served a need in that it was deployed in a context where serious debates about anthropomorphism took place among scholarly elites and general society. One can even say that such use of Ibn 'Asakir's works must have further enhanced his aura and legacy, especially among the opponents of anthropomorphism as he "equipped" them with Hadith traditions to repel it.

To conclude, I repeat a point made earlier that the sheer effort and time needed to copy, study, and teach the many works of Ibn 'Asakir, especially the *Ta'rikh* and its 800 fascicles, seem by the standards of our time beyond comprehension. Doing that repeatedly is simply inconceivable today. But the students of Ibn 'Asakir did it. For the *Ta'rikh* alone, it took them a minimum of three years to study it with him (and most of them did it twice), an equal number of years to make their own copies of it, and also an equal number of years to teach it themselves (and some of them taught it twice or more). There is no doubt that they passed certificates to some students from prestigious families without them having to sit in for such time-consuming effort. But the evidence we have demonstrates beyond any doubt that they actually sat down in the Umayyad Mosque, in the College of Hadith, in the Jarukhiyya College, and elsewhere, several days a week for three years to teach the *Ta'rikh* to large crowds. In the meantime, they were also busy teaching his other books. In doing so, they not only assured the preservation of Ibn 'Asakir's literary output, they made it central to the religious scholarship and scholarly life in Damascus, given the role the city came to play in Sunni learning. Equally important, these yeoman efforts enabled Ibn 'Asakir's legacy to spread more widely and further afield and to gain many more admirers.

IBN 'ASAKIR'S LEGACY THROUGH HIS *TA'RIKH*

Another aspect of Ibn 'Asakir's legacy relates to his *Ta'rikh* and its positive impact on the image of Damascus as one of Islam's major cities with deep roots and rich capital in terms of its contribution to Islamic history and civilization. In Chapter 4, I discussed the impact of the book on education and scholarship. Here, I address its impact in carving out a unique role for Damascus and its people in Sunnism more broadly.

With respect to scope and scale, there is nothing that comes close to Ibn 'Asakir's treatment of Damascus in his *Ta'rikh*. What is unique about it (and about Ibn 'Asakir) is that, unlike all other similar works on cities, he inspired many later scholars to continue his efforts, so much so that Damascus became the only city for which we have continuous and massive historical data on the notable scholars who were active there, and a large swathe of its history from early Islam all the way down to the twentieth century.

To illustrate, in chronological order we have: *al-Rawdatayn fi akhbar al-dawlatayn al-nuriyya wa-l-salahiyya* (*The Two Gardens Concerning the Kingdoms of Nur al-Din and Saladin*) and *Dhayl 'ala al-Rawdatayn* (*Continuation of the Two Gardens*) by Abu Shama (d. 665/1268); *al-Muqtafi 'ala Dhayl al-Rawdatayn* (*The Sequel of the Continuation of the Two Gardens*) by 'Alam al-Din al-Birzali; *al-Wafayat* (*The Obituaries*) by Taqiy al-Din Ibn Rafi' (d. 774/1372); *Dhakha'ir al-qasr fi tarajim nubala' al-'asr* (*The Palace Gems being the Biographies of the Notable Contemporaries*) by Shams al-Din Ibn Tulun (d. 953/1546); *Tarajim al-a'yan min abna' al-zaman* (*Biographies of the Notables from History*) by al-Hasan b. Muhammad al-Burini (d. 1024/1615); *al-Kawakib al-sa'ira bi-a'yan al-mi'a al-'ashira* (*The Orbiting Planets on the Notables of the Tenth Century A.H.*) by Najm al-Din al-Ghazzi (d. 1061/1651); *Khulasat al-athar fi a'yan al-qarn al-hadi 'ashar* (*Surveying the Legacy of the Notables of the Eleventh Century A.H.*) by Muhammad Amin al-Muhibbi (d. 1111/1699); *Silk al-durar fi a'yan al-qarn al-thani 'ashar* (*String of Jewels on the Notables of the Twelfth Century A.H.*) by Muhammad Khalil al-Muradi (d. 1206/1791); *Hilyat al-Bashar fi tarikh al-qarn al-thalith 'ashar* (*Ornaments of Humanity being the History of the Thirteenth Century A.H.*) by 'Abd al-Razzaq al-Bitar (d. 1335/1917); and *Muntakhab al-tawarikh li-Dimashq* (*Selected History of Damascus*) by Muhammad Adib al-Husni (d. 1359/1940).

Even though some of these books might have been initially intended as sequels to other books, they actually focus almost exclusively on the scholars of Damascus and its broader area, and as such can be seen as keeping alive the tradition that Ibn 'Asakir had started. One can also add that in their efforts to keep alive the tradition and pass it on to the following generation, they were not only inspired by him but they aspired to replicate his titanic accomplishment. Again, these efforts sustained the legacy of Ibn 'Asakir and elevated him and his scholarship to legendary status.

The most impactful aspect of this collective effort is that it created a powerful cultural and intellectual legacy for the city of Damascus, which as I will discuss in the subsequent section endowed it with a tremendous political capital, which was invested in the engineering of a modern Syrian national identity at the beginning of the twentieth century. The efforts to forge such an identity necessitated the production of books along the model of Ibn 'Asakir's *Ta'rikh* — most notably, two multi-volume works: *Muntakhab al-tawarikh li-Dimashq* by al-Husni, which appeared in three volumes between 1927 and 1934, and *Khitat al-Sham* (*Description of Damascus*) by Muhammad Kurd 'Ali (d. 1372/1953), which was published in six volumes between 1925 and 1928. In effect, both al-Husni and Kurd 'Ali plagiarized Ibn 'Asakir's *Ta'rikh* and bridged it with material from other sources all the way up to the twentieth century. Both were products for the "modern" Damascenes, but they came from the womb of Ibn 'Asakir's *Ta'rikh*.

MODERN LEGACY, SYRIAN NATIONALISM AND ISLAMIC NATIONALISM

In April of 1979, the Syrian Ministry of Higher Education organized a massive conference to celebrate the 900th birthday of Ibn 'Asakir. The speeches, historical studies, and poems that were delivered during the week-long series of events were published in a massive volume of 850 pages, entitled *Ibn 'Asakir: al-Kalimat wa-l-buhuth wa-l-qasa'id al-mulqat fi al-ihtifal bi-mu'arrikh Dimashq al-kabir fi dhikra murur tis'uma'at sana 'ala wiladatih 499–1399 H. (Ibn 'Asakir: the Speeches, Analytical Studies, and Poems Delivered during the Ceremony to Celebrate the Great Historian of Damascus on the Occasion of His 900th Birthday 499–1399 A.H.).* In every sense, the conference and the volume that came out of it represent the national and regional recognition of Ibn 'Asakir, at the official and popular levels, in Syria and in the Arab and Muslim worlds. In conjunction with the conference, the Lebanese publishing house Dar al-Masira reprinted the seven volumes of Badran's *Tahdhib*, the partial abridgment of Ibn 'Asakir's *Ta'rikh* done earlier in the twentieth century.

Also, in conjunction with the massive gathering, the Syrian government named a major avenue in Damascus in honor of Ibn 'Asakir (Ibn Assaker Street according to the dual-language sign that was posted by the municipality of the city). It circles Old Damascus for more than three kilometers, from north of Bab Tuma (St. Thomas Gate) on the northeast side, to Bab al-Musalla (the Prayer Mosque Gate) on the southwest near Bab al-Saghir (the Small Gate) cemetery where Ibn

'Asakir was buried. There was also a public park named after him (*Hadiqat Ibn 'Asakir*), which is adjacent to the southern end of the street.

No other scholarly figure from Syria's distant past received anything similar to this exceptional and coordinated attention. The question that begs itself is what explains such recognition given to a medieval scholar? The answer lies in the birth of several movements of reform in the early twentieth century that were tied to broad forms of Syrian nationalism – especially Pan-Arab Nationalism and Pan-Islamic nationalism – all of which saw in Ibn 'Asakir a great model to "resurrect" for modern generations. More importantly, they identified his *Ta'rikh* as a great resource that, in their judgment, proved the legitimacy of their claims for Syria as a political nation state.

Therefore, the event and initiatives underscore the political and cultural significance of Ibn 'Asakir in the modern Syrian national and Arabo-Islamic consciousness. After all, they expressed and represented the views of a wide spectrum of the political, educational, intellectual, and social intelligentsia in Syria and the region, who viewed Ibn 'Asakir with contemporary eyes and through the prism of modern needs. In other words, we are talking about the exploitation of Ibn 'Asakir, which is part of a much wider process of the exploitation of history and historical figures that is not limited to Arab and Islamic history and historical figures, but can be seen in all modern cultures and polities as well.

THE LATE-NINETEENTH- TO EARLY TWENTIETH-CENTURY CONTEXT

As discussed in Chapter 4, the Damascene Hanbali scholar 'Abd al-Qadir Badran started working on an abridged edition of Ibn 'Asakir's *Ta'rikh* in the first decade of the twentieth century, and the first volume of the *Tahdhib* was published in 1911 by Rawdat al-Sham Press. The renowned local newspaper *al-Muqtabas* (which was owned by Muhammad Kurd 'Ali) announced on its pages the publication of Badran's *Tahdhib* in the following words:

You cannot find a person who knows the history of Islam but yearns
badly for the publication of the book on the history of Damascus by the
great Hadith-memorizer Ibn 'Asakir, who died in 571 H. At last, shaykh
'Abd al-Qadir Badran, one of Damascus's righteous people, had the will
power and is publishing it. He indeed produced an edition of it in 128
pages, where the repetitions have been removed as well as the chains of
transmission... We would love, however, for the editor to publish all of
this massive work, which extends to eighty volumes exactly in the way
its author had written it, even though it was in the style of the Hadith
scholars and not that of chroniclers. It would be even fine to publish
one of the abridgments that were done by a notable scholar of old...
Nevertheless, the circulation of the book in this form might encourage
our sons and grandsons in the coming years to publish what Ibn 'Asakir
wrote in its entirety.

(al-Muqtabas 66 [1 August 1911])

A year later, when the second volume of Badran's *Tahdhib* came out,
journalist 'Abd al-Fattah al-Sukkari penned the following words in an
editorial in *al-Muqtabas*:

Years have passed and researchers and the educated among the readers
have yearned to see in their hands the *Ta'rikh Dimashq* by the Hadith-
memorizer Ibn 'Asakir. However, the enormity of the work, given
the repetitions and the many chains of transmission – which was the
habit of Hadith scholars – discouraged publishers from publishing it.
Finally, last year God delegated for this task Khalid Qarasli, the owner
of Rawdat al-Sham Press, and he started printing the *Ta'rikh Dimashq*
in Damascus... This book, given the renown of its author, will surely
benefit a large public... and owning a copy of it is indispensable for
passionate readers who seek to learn the history of this capital and
its men whose fame spread far and wide. We thank the publisher
immensely for taking on such a task at a time when those who support
knowledge and literatures and who study history have become a rarity.
Indeed, you find most people have become preoccupied with the present
and the future, and thus inattentive to the past. Alas, how can one
succeed in his present if he is oblivious of his past!

(al-Muqtabas 81 [1 November 1912])

In these two pieces, which were followed by other similar pieces
in *al-Muqtabas* (and possibly other newspapers as well), we see the

tremendous emphasis placed on how Ibn 'Asakir's *Ta'rikh* allows modern Syrians to learn about their past in order to shape their present and
future. Al-Sukkari's words "how can one succeed in his present if he is
oblivious of his past!" indicate the kind of history early Syrian nationalists at the beginning of the twentieth century were eager to diffuse in
order to shape Syrian national identity and historical memory. Hence,
the yearning of everyone who knows history is fulfilled by the publication of the *Ta'rikh*, even if it is in an abridged edition. For those who
do not, "owning a copy of it is indispensable... to learn the history of
this capital and its men whose fame spread far and wide."

Indeed, Ibn 'Asakir and his *Ta'rikh* were essential for the engineering
of a new Syrian historical memory and national identity by advocates
who played a major role in religious and secular education, journal-
ism, theatre, society, and political life. As such, the *Ta'rikh* was fundamental for the integration of specific historical and religious memory
that made the construction of this new national identity possible
and popular (irrespective of whether these efforts were state-based,
ethnic-based, or religious-based).

Ibn 'Asakir was the go-to historical figure for some early Syrian
nationalists because his *Ta'rikh* provided the key historical building
blocks for their project. He appealed to them because of two traits:
he was a Sunni Muslim from Damascus and he, in their opinion, advocated Syrian nationalism. The former aspect is very important because
most of the Syrian nationalists were also Sunni Muslims (at least cul-
turally), and cared to shape Syrian nationalism within the broader
context of Sunni Islam as a civilization and Arabic as a language and
culture. The second trait needs no explanation, only that Ibn 'Asakir's
medieval geographic patriotism – his attachment to *Bilad al-Sham* as
the locus of Islamic sacred history – was not what modern political
nationalists promoted, but this was not an issue of concern for them
because they conflated the two.

It is important to explain the complexity of the nationalist scene
in Syria at the time. In the first two decades of the twentieth century, Syria was not yet a clearly defined political entity. Even the
word Syria was not yet *au courant*. What was widely used to refer to
Syria was the expression *Bilad al-Sham*, or simply *al-Sham* (*al-Sham*

was also used interchangeably to mean Damascus), and it denoted the broad geographic span that extended from modern-day southern Jordan to Syria's northern borders with Turkey, and from the eastern desert separating Syria from Iraq to the Mediterranean Sea in the west. Thus, *Bilad al-Sham* included what is today Lebanon, Palestine, Israel, Jordan, Syria (except the part north and east of the Euphrates which was known as *al-Jazira*, or Upper Mesopotamia), and the region of Antioch in Turkey. Throughout Islamic history, *Bilad al-Sham* remained a geographical concept and never became a political concept, even under the Ottomans, who divided it into several administrative units; Damascus was the seat of a governorate, and there were a few others as well (e.g., Aleppo, Acre, Beirut).

Therefore, when one talks about Syrian nationalism at the beginning of the twentieth century, we should not understand it as something tied to an existing polity. Rather, it was fluid, and it encompassed various movements, each eager to shape greater Syria, or a part of it, as a political entity with historical roots in Islam, Arab culture, the ancient Near East, and so on.

The early Syrian nationalists who were drawn to Ibn 'Asakir believed in the unity of *Bilad al-Sham*, and advocated an Arabo-Syrian or Islamo-Syrian form of nationalism, whereby Syria was seen as the leading political entity of a pan-Arab or pan-Islamic polity. Moreover, and with the exception of a few cases, most of these Syrian nationalists at that time were simultaneously involved in several camps, and that was possible because all options – i.e., forms of Pan-Arabism and Pan-Islamism – were still viable. Hence, the diversity of nationalist discourses, most of which shared a specific historical memory and identity that could be easily deployed in any one of these discourses. Once Syria was declared a state by the League of Nations in 1920 and placed under a French mandate, and Lebanon, Trans-Jordan, and Palestine were carved out as separate entitites, Syrian nationalism became further complicated by this new reality, especially regarding the "how" and "against what" the identity of this new Syria was to be shaped and defined. Not to mention the many early Syrian nationalists who remained (partially at least) against it and loyal to their old ideologies, including the unity of *Bilad al-Sham*.

Throughout this transitional period, Ibn 'Asakir's *Ta'rikh* maintained its relevance. As mentioned earlier, a serious pursuit to publish it was unleashed at the beginning of the twentieth century, except that the book was massive, which presented – and remained throughout the twentieth century – a logistical problem. Yet, it is the nightmare of publishing Ibn 'Asakir's *Ta'rikh* that makes us realize how significant he was for the engineering of the Syrian national identity and historical memory and how desperate different groups of nationalists were to publish it. The task had to be done at any cost, that is by hook or by crook (to borrow the expression of the medieval English scholastic John Wycliffe).

To return to an important point made earlier, Ibn 'Asakir's own engagement with Syrian patriotism was different from that of modern Syrian nationalists in the twentieth century. At least in one major aspect, the two diverge in a big way. Ibn 'Asakir's patriotism about Syria or *Bilad al-Sham* had no political characteristics. It was a geographical particularism tied to a salvific mission. The tendency of many Muslims in pre-modern times to emphasize the sense of belonging and attachment to a homeland (*watan*) has already been examined and highlighted by several scholars (for instance, Zayde Antrim's *Routes & Realms: The Power of Place in the Early Muslim World*), and Ibn 'Asakir's patriotism fits perfectly into that. The modern nationalists played on this ambiguity, and channeled Ibn 'Asakir away from his apolitical geographical particularism and into the fray of their own highly political nationalism.

Moreover, Ibn 'Asakir and his *Ta'rikh* resonated with Syrian society – and Arab society in general – precisely because he was already very familiar to them, especially supporters of Arabo-Syrian or Islamo-Syrian nationalism. In other words, the Arabo-Islamic heritage furnished, in the imagination of many Syrian political activists, a glue for Syrian national cohesion, and offered a point of agreement between various competing nationalist movements (pan-Islamic, Arabo-Islamic, pan-Arab, Arabo-Syrian, Islamo-Syrian, etc.), precisely because each movement saw in this heritage things it could use for its discourse. The significance and uniqueness of Ibn 'Asakir's *Ta'rikh* was that it allowed them not only to employ it as a documentary source for

Syria's history, but to point to it as one of the first books that, in their opinion, validated Syria as a political entity.

Influential figures at the time – such as Muhammad Kurd 'Ali who was of Kurdish background and oscillated between Pan-Arabism and Arabo-Islamism, and many others – lifted from the Arabo-Islamic heritage events, texts, and personalities and choreographed them into a historical memory, which resonated with the broader Syrian society throughout the twentieth century. Again, the general familiarity with these events, texts, and personalities was a key factor that assured positive acceptability and success of this effort. Kurd 'Ali in particular was a pioneer who played a significant role in the "resurrection" and publication of specific texts from the medieval Arabo-Islamic canon and specific historical "role models", precisely to provide a foundation for the construction of a Syrian national memory and identity shaped by the Arabo-Islamic culture. Along with his *Khitat al-Sham*, which was modeled along and plagiarized a good part of Ibn 'Asakir's *Ta'rikh*, Kurd 'Ali was also directly involved in the publication of the *Ta'rikh*. As head of the newly formed Arab Scientific Academy of Damascus (*al-Majma' al-'Ilmi al-'Arabi bi-Dimashq*) in 1919 – which was renamed in 1958 as the Academy of Arabic Language of Damascus (*Majma' al-Lugha al-'Arabiyya bi-Dimashq*) – Kurd 'Ali pushed for the publication of Ibn 'Asakir's *Ta'rikh*. He even handpicked a team of young scholars to collect its manuscripts and edit them.

Here are Kurd 'Ali's words about the *Ta'rikh* and the importance of Ibn 'Asakir, which he expressed in his *Kunuz al-ajdad* (*Treasures of Our Ancestors*), a book containing short biographies for fifty-one famous Muslim figures, from Ibn al-Muqaffa' (d. c. 139/756) to Ibn Khaldun (d. 808/1406); interestingly, all of them were Sunnis except for Ibn al-Muqaffa' (the famous author of *Kalila wa-Dimna*, who held Manichaean beliefs):

> Every student finds in it what he seeks. People could avail themselves of a book because they find the same thing or close to it in similar books. With the *Ta'rikh Dimashq*, however, no educated person can do without it, taking it as a companion and delightful resource, depending on it to acquire knowledge about the lives of those who once had noble status in this society. He [Ibn 'Asakir] borrowed from those who came before

him, and fate had it that some of these sources were lost. If it were not
for him quoting them in his enjoyable book, a massive amount of the
knowledge about the lives of many of these men would have been lost,
and with that, the history of this nation would have been lost.

(Kurd 'Ali, *Kunuz al-ajdad* 311)

Thus, Ibn 'Asakir's *Ta'rikh* offered an indispensable window into the
glorious history of Syria. Without it, no one can call himself or her-
self truly educated. Without it, the history of the Arabs and Syria is
incomplete.

We find a similar view expressed by Salah al-Din al-Munajjid, a
protégé of Kurd 'Ali and the editor of the first two volumes of Ibn
'Asakir's *Ta'rikh*. In his introduction to the first volume, al-Munajjid
penned:

> Damascus never saw in its entire history a Hadith scholar, who surpassed
> the great memorizer in Hadith transmission. Nor did it encounter an author
> who compiled eighty volumes on its history other than he. It suffices her the
> honor of having the most massive history written about an Islamic city by an
> author who was one of the prominent scholars in Islam... This *Ta'rikh* has
> an eminence that other books could not attain, for it is an immense treasure
> of Arabic culture. It is the broadest book ever written on Damascus and
> most inclusive. No book like it with such a breadth and comprehensiveness
> was written before, and no one after he ever wrote on the histories of cities
> the way Ibn 'Asakir did. This *Ta'rikh* will remain in the Arabic culture one
> of a kind, no other book compares to it.

(Ibn 'Asakir, *Ta'rikh* 1: 31)

Yet, Kurd 'Ali was also critical of the kind of material one finds in the
Ta'rikh. He argued:

> The author recounted stories, which we think he did not believe were
> true. The intellect has the capacity to closely examine and dismiss
> falsehood. For which of the books of the scholars of Hadith and the
> predecessors is safe from our criticism and probing? Therefore, with
> an intellect like that of Ibn 'Asakir, it is impossible that he could have
> believed the myths and legends that were cited in the introductory
> volumes of the *Ta'rikh*, given that he was the most knowledgeable
> scholar about the weak and fabricated hadiths.

(Kurd 'Ali, *Kunuz al-ajdad* 312–313)

It is clear that Kurd 'Ali did not approve of some of the material that one finds in Ibn 'Asakir's *Ta'rikh*; he meant specifically the hadiths and legendary anecdotes about the sanctity of Syria and many spots in and around Damascus. It is also evident that he avoided criticizing him directly, contending that Ibn 'Asakir wrote according to the historical tradition and conventions of his time. Today, Kurd 'Ali added, thanks to Ibn Khaldun history has become a science, and historians openly question these myths and prove their falsehood.

The irony is that despite this subtle criticism, it was precisely the introductory volumes of Ibn 'Asakir *Ta'rikh* and not the subsequent volumes (which essentially contain very little to offer on the history of Syria per se) that served Kurd 'Ali's political objectives and those of nationalists like him. So, it is safe to argue that Kurd 'Ali was pre-empting any criticism of himself, all the while realizing that those myths and legends that he was "dismissing" as irrational formed the meat for the Arabo-Islamic nationalist identity and historical memory that he was helping to construct for Syria, and assured the success of the political endeavor among the masses. In other words, Kurd 'Ali wanted, as the 3rd Duke of Norfolk once avowed, to have his cake and eat it too.

It should be emphasized, however, that even though the effort to publish Ibn 'Asakir's *Ta'rikh* did not fully succeed during the first half of the twentieth century, the hubbub around it made it an indispensable reference for everyone interested in writing on the history of Damascus and Syria, further endearing it and its author exponentially to an educated public. Even more, the *Ta'rikh* soared in the public imagination of Syrians in general precisely because those who abridged it or quoted it insisted on "cleansing" it from boring repetitions and chains of transmission as well as the absurd legends and myths, as Badran and Kurd 'Ali advocated. This "cleaner" look made the *Ta'rikh* even more attractive and desirable to a picky intelligentsia. In particular, selecting chunks of "clean" material from it and featuring them in countless large and small books intended for different types of educated masses made Ibn 'Asakir into a giant of a historian, to whose colossal effort modern Syrians owed some of their history.

To emphasize, these books were meant to showcase the beauty and richness of Damascus, its charming suburbs, rivers, mosques, bathhouses, etc., and they were part of a massive effort tied to the presentation of the city as the capital of the new Syria. Hence, we find in the 1920s the multi-volume works of Kurd 'Ali (*Khitat al-Sham*) and al-Husni (*Muntakhab al-tawarikh li-Dimashq*), mentioned earlier, as well as smaller ones, such as *Jabal Qasyun* (*Mount Qasyun*) which came out in 1946 by Muhammad Ahmad Dahman (d. 1409/1988), *Khitat Dimashq* (*Topography of Damascus*) in 1949 by al-Munajjid, and *Ghutat Dimashq* (*The Ghuta Ramparts of Damascus*) in 1949 also by Kurd 'Ali (it was republished in a revised edition in 1952), to name a few. As "modern" and "scientific" histories, they and many other books like them became the new canon for the educated masses from which to learn about the history and topography of their city. Collectively, they furnished the modern Syrian at the time with a historical identity and memory for their capital city, and by extension they helped shape the new Syrian national identity and historical memory. And since they lifted some of their material from Ibn 'Asakir's *Ta'rikh*, the latter assumed a role in the creation of this new historical identity and memory. As the sentiments quoted above clearly convey, the *Ta'rikh* became a bedrock for national identity, thus further fueling the desire to have it published. Therefore, that the actual publication of the *Ta'rikh* dragged on for years (however interesting the details of that might be as a historical curiosity) is beside the point and does not convey a lack of enthusiasm or appreciation for its significance. The book was living and exerting influence in other forms.

As an aside, this energy around Ibn 'Asakir and his *Ta'rikh* also drew some French historians to work on the *Ta'rikh* (largely due to their colonial presence in Syria and Lebanon). In 1942–1943, Michel Écochard and Claude Le Cœur published an architectural history entitled *Les bains de Damas* (*The Bathhouses of Damascus*). More importantly, Nikita Elisséeff (1915–1997) – originally a Russian immigrant from St. Petersburg and Secretary General of the French Institute in Damascus – made a translation of the two volumes of the *Ta'rikh* edited by al-Munajjid, which he entitled *La description de Damas d'Ibn 'Asakir* (*The Description of Damascus by Ibn 'Asakir*), and which came out in 1959. This led to a growing interest in Ibn 'Asakir on the part of scholars in Europe and North America. The other wave of interest happened in the late 1980s following the issue of a photostat edition of the Zahiriyya manuscript (Zahiriyya A in Chapter 4) of the *Ta'rikh* by Dar al-Basha'ir in Amman, Jordan. The most recent wave began when Dar al-Fikr published the entire work starting in 1996.

THE LATE-TWENTIETH-CENTURY CONTEXT

The massive conference convened by the Syrian government in 1979 to celebrate the 900th birthday of Ibn 'Asakir, discussed above, happened at a significant date. The Iranian revolution and the Soviet invasion of Afghanistan had occurred a few months earlier. The attention to Ibn 'Asakir awakened new interest in him and his writings, given the new context. He became an inspirational figure for Islamized nationalism. This development is significant given that in the 1970s, Arab nationalism started to lose traction among some Syrian elites and public (and elsewhere in the Arab world as well), and gave way to a rising current of Islamism that pushed for the Islamization of Syrian nationalism. This process happened in other Arab and Muslim countries as well, such as Egypt, Algeria, and Turkey. Some of the interest was also fueled by Salafi missionaries sponsored by the Kingdom of Saudi Arabia, who looked at Ibn 'Asakir with the same reverential eyes as medieval scholars but with minds saturated with the politics of the moment. Thus, the choreographed national memory and identity engineered by Syrian nationalists at the beginning of the twentieth century morphed into a Syrian Islamic national identity and memory. This was partly a natural progression, given the fact that the Syrian national identity was already saturated with Islamic resonances and symbolisms.

Yet, there was a major difference between the Islamized Syrian nationalism of the late twentieth century and the Arabo- and Islamo-Syrian nationalism of the early twentieth century, in that the latter was tied either to a cultural Islamic heritage or to an equally broad pan-Islamic discourse, sometimes with partial secularism. The current

Islamization of Syrian nationalism is tied to a very specific Islamist political discourse that completely rejects secularism and focuses first and foremost on the Islamization of countries, rather than the creation of a pan-Islamic polity (even if this remains a distant objective predicated on the success of the Islamization process).

Equally, the historically unacceptable material in Ibn 'Asakir's books, which was rejected by early nationalists, was especially appealing for this new wave of Syrian Islamists and Salafists. For them, it provides a treasure trove they considered essential for their religious and political project. The "questionable" hadiths and "far-fetched" legends teach dogma, and are therefore inseparable from Islamic history. Moreover, the chains of transmission and frequent repetitions of the same hadiths furnish a priceless window into a time when the Muslims vied among each other to transmit the words of their Prophet in minute detail. As such, Ibn 'Asakir reminded them of the importance of real knowledge and how it is to be pursued.

Moreover, Ibn 'Asakir is especially appealing to this Islamist and Salafist discourse, because he was a pioneer who pushed for the revivification of Sunnism and lived and wrote during the Crusader period when Syria was under attack by medieval European invaders. As such, they could turn him into an "advocate" for modern jihad and a supporter of modern Islamists and Salafists who are also aspiring to "revivify" Sunnism against western domination. Ibn 'Asakir's religious books that championed the hegemonic revivification of Sunnism in Syria and Egypt were "rediscovered", and became the subject of serious attention as well because they could be employed in anti-Shi'i (and anti-Iran) rhetoric. Hence, we see the growing interest in treatises and books written by Ibn 'Asakir on jihad and polemical topics, which were completely ignored by the earlier nationalists.

We also see a significant increase in the number of books and studies on Ibn 'Asakir's religious advocacy, such as the publication in 1991 of *Ibn 'Asakir wa-dawruh fi al-jihad didd al-salibiyyin fi 'ahd al-dawlatayn al-nuriyya wa-l-ayyubiyya (Ibn 'Asakir and His Role in Jihad against the Crusaders during the Zangid and Ayyubid Sultanates)*. The author, a Syrian historian named Ahmad Halwani, described his feelings when he started researching Ibn 'Asakir in the following manner:

> I sensed that I had in front of me a leading pioneer scholar who lived
> in a historical period similar to the one in which we live. This scholar
> lived during a time when our nation witnessed a crusading onslaught
> that came to nest in the Arab countries. Facing it were dismembered
> and divided small Arab states who were incapable of unity and facing the
> colonial occupation due to petty greed of rule, intrigues, deceptions,
> hypocrisy, and futile interests. This great scholar, however, did not only
> reject this reality. He committed himself to face it, challenge it, and
> work to change it. His plan to achieve that was a transparent cultural
> mobilization to all members of society… He allied himself with Sultan
> Nur al-Din. Even more, he, like any true scholar, pushed him to achieve
> the unity of Syria and Egypt, as a first step in preparation for attacking
> the Crusader colonies.
>
> (Halwani, *Ibn 'Asakir* 11–12)

Halwani continued:

> Circumstances have it that our Arab nation lives through similar
> conditions to those during which our scholar Ibn 'Asakir lived. Our
> nation is facing an Israeli Zionist conquest in occupied Palestine,
> while divisions, intrigues and lies drill through its body. Hypocrisy is
> widespread. What we lack is the initiative, with good intention, to
> accomplish what we have started at the beginning of the modern Arab
> Awakening in terms of resisting colonization, fighting the battle of
> independence, continuing the struggle to accomplish the Arab unity…
>
> (Halwani, *Ibn 'Asakir* 12–13)

In the words of Halwani, Ibn 'Asakir is valuable for him and his modern Arabo-Muslim audience because he is a model for them. The time
in which he lived is similar to their time. The challenges then were as
monumental as they are now: internal division and external schemes
to take away the Arabs' land and its resources. Therefore, he can give
them a road map to follow, so that they can know how to get out of
the current state of weakness and subjugation.

No doubt, the language of Halwani resonated with some nostalgic
forms of Arabo-Islamic nationalism. This is not the case, however,
with the Syrian Salafist Muhammad Muti' al-Hafiz, who a few years
later published a book on Ibn 'Asakir in which he expressed similar
sentiments but with a much more Islamic overtone:

The great memorizer witnessed the fragmentation of the Muslim world and its division into smaller states... In brief, the Muslim community experienced at the time of Ibn 'Asakir something similar to what we see today in terms of other nations ruling over it, conquering it either intellectually or militarily, causing its fragmentation... In the face of this, Ibn 'Asakir realized that the only way to get rid of this weakness and turmoil was through the invocation of jihad in the path of God. He also found that the only way to achieve the jihad was by preparing people, spiritually and scientifically, warning them about the danger around them, for they have seen it firsthand several times, such as when the Crusaders laid siege to Damascus and were on the verge of committing in it what they committed in Jerusalem. He also realized that the only way to achieve both goals was by dissemination of the noble prophetic Hadith and the lessons of history.

(al-Hafiz, *al-Hafiz Ibn 'Asakir* 11–12)

Here, in the words of al-Hafiz, Islam and the Muslim community replace the Arab and Arab land of Halwani. Ibn 'Asakir's pioneering role in cultural mobilization, in the words of Halwani, becomes the spiritual and scientific preparation of people, in the words of al-Hafiz. Al-Hafiz also argued that Ibn 'Asakir knew that the only way to achieve his objective was through the dissemination of Hadith, which is an indication that Islam's and the Muslim community's revival today needs the dissemination of Hadith.

Clearly then, the language we read in the words of the likes of Halwani and al-Hafiz is different from that used by the nationalists at the beginning of the twentieth century. This is to be expected as each group used Ibn 'Asakir for different ends. At the beginning of the twentieth century, Ibn 'Asakir was championed for his "contribution" to the formation of Syrian national identity. However, this was not sufficient for those at the end of the twentieth century who were drawn more to Ibn 'Asakir as an advocate of jihad and as a religious reformer, but less so as a medieval geo-nationalist forerunner.

At any rate, this modern fascination with Ibn 'Asakir is in some ways similar to Ibn 'Asakir's own fascination with the Islamic past. His ideological outlook drove him to rehabilitate Islamic history and personalities in ways that lent themselves to a political and religious project he was helping to define. He read history backward and designed it by deploying countless prophetic hadiths, historical accounts, and legends in what proved to be a superbly effective way for his audience. The modernists, too, read Islamic and Arab history backward from the perspectives of their own modern concerns and needs. They deemed Ibn 'Asakir – and some other figures as well – to be crucial for the development of modern national and religious identities, and thus retooled him and others in the most effective way to serve their concerns and needs. It might be far-fetched to say history repeats itself, but it is eerily déjà vu.

GLOSSARY

Abbasids: The name of a dynasty of Caliphs who removed the Umayyads in 132/750 and ruled from Baghdad (except for the first twelve years when their capital was Kufa). Around the middle of the third/ninth century, they championed Sunnism. Between the mid-fourth/tenth century and until they were destroyed by the Mongols in 656/1258, they were hegemonized by powerful sultans (first the Shi'i Buyids and then the Sunni Seljuks). Around 659/1261, they were reinstated in Cairo, but only as puppets for the Mamluks, and they were completely dissolved by the Ottomans in 923/1517.

Amir: A title given to a ruler or a member of a notable political family in the premodern Muslim world. From it, the English term *emir* comes, which specifically means "prince," and thus has a narrower meaning than *amir*. It was also used as a title for a military commander.

Ash'aris: The theological school named after the Sunni theologian Abu al-Hasan al-Ash'ari (d. 324/936), and which became one of the most dominant schools of theology in Sunni Islam.

Companions: The followers of the Prophet Muhammad who were his contemporaries (in Arabic, *al-Sahaba*). Generally, they came to signify the best generation of Muslims. Given their role in the first civil wars and schisms among Muslims, Sunnis and Shi'is disagree on who among the Companions was righteous and who was not. As "preservers" of the Hadith of Muhammad, they were treated as saints.

Fatimids: A dynasty of Isma'ili Shi'i Caliphs who emerged in North Africa in the beginning of the third/ninth century, conquered Egypt in 358/969, and established the city of Cairo. From there, they expanded to Syria and the Hijaz (Mecca and Medina). Saladin ended their state in 566/1171.

Hadith: The corpus constituting the words and deeds attributed to the Prophet Muhammad and the anecdotes his followers told about him. They were transmitted by many of his Companions and are documented in a wide variety of books. The term is also used to mean the individual accounts constituting this corpus.

Hanafis: One of the largest branches of Sunni jurisprudence, named after the early jurist Abu Hanifa (d. 150/767). It was very popular among Turkic peoples, especially the Seljuks. It did not have many followers in Syria and Egypt until the Seljuk invasion. Its popularity in the Arab world in particular is due to the Ottoman Empire whose official legal practice was Hanafism.

Hanbalis: A branch of Sunni jurisprudence which is the strictest in terms of adherence to the Sunna of Muhammad with a good dose of literalism in their interpretation of the Qur'an. They were the second largest community in Damascus at the time of Ibn 'Asakir, and always represented a challenge to the Shafi'is.

Ijaza: Certificate given to a student to teach and transmit a certain book on the authority of the teacher. It is comparable to the successful completion of a college course today. Ideally, an *ijaza* was granted on the basis of actual study with the teacher, but gradually disciples from well-known families were able to receive *ijaza*s by written correspondence with a teacher, which was considered inferior to the former.

Isma'ilis: A Shi'i sect, which emerged in the late second/eighth century. In the fifth/eleventh century, the sect split in two as a result of a schism concerning which of two Fatimid brothers had the right of succession; this gave rise to the Nizari Isma'ilis, who started as a minority and counted among their ranks a militant group (famously known in English as Assassins). The fall of the Fatimids in 566/1171 brought an almost complete end to their form of Isma'ilism, and opened the way for the Nizaris to become the dominant force in Isma'ilism until today.

Al-Jazira: The northern part of historical Mesopotamia, often referred to as Upper Mesopotamia, wedged between the Euphrates and the Tigris rivers. Its main city was Edessa (*al-Ruha* in Arabic, and *Urfa* in Turkish). Today, it is split between southeast Turkey, northeast Syria, and northwest Iraq.

Madrasa: In the medieval Islamic period a *madrasa* (literally meaning a school) was something comparable to a college today. A *madrasa* often had a main professor and several assistants, and specialized in a specific field. Each *madrasa* was generally endowed to assure its survival beyond the life of the benefactor. They ranged from a single-room structure to a large compound with a courtyard, rooms for study and lodging, a prayer room, and a garden.

Majlis: A seminar on a specific topic usually held in a mosque or a college. Typically, the students sat facing the teacher, who lectured about a topic or read a book to them, often with the help of an assistant. Generally, the students wanting to receive a certificate (*ijaza*) from the teacher would have had a chance to copy the book ahead of the class, bring it with them, and make sure it matched what they heard from their teacher.

Malikis: A branch of Sunni jurisprudence named after Malik b. Anas (d. 179/795), the author of *Kitab al-Muwatta'* (*The Trodden Path*). At the time of Ibn 'Asakir, they formed a visible minority in Damascus and Egypt.

Maturidis: A Sunni school of theology founded by al-Maturidi (d. 333/944). It became widespread among Turkic peoples in Central

Asia and was introduced into the Middle East with the coming of the
Seljuks and their warlords.

Mufti: A high-ranking authority in Islamic law who furnishes legal
opinions and rulings, and also settles legal disputes within and between
branches of jurisprudence.

Al-Musawat: A peculiarity of Hadith transmission to brag about,
whereby a much later Hadith scholar, such as Ibn 'Asakir's teacher
al-Furawi (d. 530/1136), could say that he possessed chains of transmission for certain hadiths featuring the same number of informants
as those quoted by the authors of the most prestigious early books of
Hadith, such as al-Bukhari (d. 256/870) and Muslim (d. 261/875),
who lived centuries before him. To give an example, al-Furawi
related a hadith where there were six informants between him and the
Prophet, and the same hadith is quoted by al-Bukhari or Muslim, who
also had six informants separating them from the Prophet. Another
name for this type is *al-'Awali.*

Mu'tazila: A famous school of rational theology in medieval Islam.
It originated in the second/eighth century as a loose movement but
crystallized around a fixed theology in the third/ninth century. Its
members were mostly Sunnis, but due to systematic persecution in
the fifth/eleventh and sixth/twelfth centuries, they became outcasts
from Sunnism. Most of their theological doctrines were borrowed by
some Shi'i groups (especially Twelvers and Zaydis).

Quraysh: The tribe that inhabited Mecca during Muhammad's
time. Its members have enjoyed great prestige and the Caliphate was
believed to be exclusive to them.

Seljuks: A dynasty of Sunni Turkic warlords from Central Asia who
invaded the Muslim world starting in the fifth/eleventh century,
occupied Baghdad in 447/1055, and put an end to the rule of the Shi'i
Buyid dynasty. They imposed themselves for close to two centuries as

the most feared sultans of Islam, and pursued a policy of Sunnification against mostly Shi'i groups, especially in Iraq and Iran.

Shafi'is: One of the most famous branches of Sunni jurisprudence, which counted among its members a large number of the Sunni masses in Syria and Egypt since the fourth/tenth century, and had an extensive network of legal scholars and judges. It was named after jurist al-Shafi'i (d. 204/820).

Shi'is: An Islamic sect, which emphasized the need to acknowledge the holy lineage of the Prophet Muhammad through his cousin and son-in-law 'Ali b. Abu Talib (d. 40/661) as divinely designated leaders (imams) of the Muslims; hence their theological disagreement with the Sunnis who contested their claim. With time, the sect split into several subsects, due to disagreement over who is the legitimate son to succeed a deceased imam. They include the Twelvers, Isma'ilis, and Zaydis, among others. The Twelvers and two forms of Isma'ilis existed in Damascus at the time of Ibn 'Asakir.

Substitutes: *Abdal* in Arabic. This is a collective reference to a group of seventy early Muslim individuals. They include Companions and Successors of the Prophet Muhammad, and according to Sunni belief they are exemplars and do God's work, and every time one of them dies, he/she is replaced with another Substitute.

Successors: The generation of Muslims who came after the Companions of the Prophet Muhammad, and did not have a chance to meet him. They learned about him from the Companions. They are revered by Muslims, although Sunnis and Shi'is each have their preferred and cursed ones.

Sunna: Literally, the conduct set forth by the Prophet Muhammad, which we read about in the Hadith. Sometimes, it is interchangeable with Hadith.

Sunni: The largest sect in Islam. It divides into several branches, each with its own system of jurisprudence (Shari'a). The five that existed at the time of Ibn 'Asakir were the Hanafis, Malikis, Shafi'is, Hanbalis, and Zahiris. It also includes several theological schools, notably, Ash'aris, Maturidis, Hanbalis, and Mu'tazila.

Umayyads: A dynasty of Caliphs who ruled the Muslim world from their capital in Damascus between 40/661 and 132/750 (after that the dynasty only survived in Muslim Spain until 423/1031). They introduced major religious reforms and dogmatic initiatives that transformed Islam and made it a global religion. The family of Ibn 'Asakir's mother traced its origin to them, which bestowed on its members tremendous social significance in a city like Damascus.

Zawiya: A designated corner inside a building, typically inside a mosque or in a mosque courtyard, which became known as a meeting place for the teaching of certain subjects.

BIBLIOGRAPHY

IBN 'ASAKIR'S BOOKS

Al-Arba'un al-abdal al-'awali. Ed. M. N. al-'Ajami. Beirut: Dar al-Basha'ir, 2004.

Al-Arba'un al-buldaniyya. Ed. 'A. al-Hariri. Beirut: al-Maktab al-Islami, 1993.

Al-Arba'un hadith fi al-hathth 'ala al-jihad. In S. A. Mourad and J. E. Lindsay. *The Intensification and Reorientation of Sunni Jihad Ideology in the Crusader Period: Ibn 'Asakir (1105–1176) of Damascus and His Age; with an edition and translation of Ibn 'Asakir's* The Forty Hadiths for Inciting Jihad. Leiden: Brill, 2013, pp. 130–203.

Al-Arba'un al-musawat. Ed. T. Bu-Srayh. Riyadh: Maktabat al-Rushd, 2003.

Hadith Ibn Jurayj. Ms. Zahiriyya *majmu'* 24, ff. 117–135.

Al-Ishraf 'ala ma'rifat al-atraf. Vol. 1. Ms. Islamic University of Medina 497.

Kitab al-Tajrid. Vol. 4. Ms. Zahiriyya *majmu'* 10, ff. 13–27.

Mu'jam al-shuyukh. 3 vols. Ed. W. Taqiy al-Din. Damascus: Dar al-Basha'ir, 2000.

Mu'jam shuyukh al-Bukhari wa-Muslim wa-Abi Dawud wa-Abi 'Isa al-Tirmidhi wa-Abi 'Abd al-Rahman al-Nasa'i, wa-Abi 'Abd Allah al-Qazwini. Ms. Khalidiyya Library of Jerusalem 1190.

Tabyin al-imtinan bi-l-amr bi-l-ikhtitan. Ed. M. F. al-Sayyid. Tanta: Dar al-Sahaba li-l-Turath, 1989.

Tabyin kahdhib al-muftari fima nasab ila al-imam Abi al-Hasan al-Ash'ari. Ed. H.-D. al-Qudsi. Damascus: Matba'at al-Tawfiq, 1928.

Tartib asma' al-sahaba al-ladhin akhraj hadithahum Ahmad Ibn Hanbal fi al-Musnad. Ed. 'A. H. Sabri. Damascus: Dar al-Basha'ir, 1989.

Ta'rikh madinat Dimashq. 57 vols. Several editors. Damascus: Majma' al-Lugha al-'Arabiyya, 1951–2020.

Ta'rikh madinat Dimashq. 80 vols. Eds. 'U. al-'Amrawi and 'A. Shiri. Beirut: Dar al-Fikr, 1995–2001.

Ta'ziyat al-muslim 'an akhih. Ed. M. F. al-Sayyid. Jidda: Maktabat al-Sahaba, 1991.

Transcribed Seminars (Majalis)

Majlis 14: *Fi dhamm man la ya'mal bi-'ilmih.* In *Majlisan min majalis al-hafiz Ibn 'Asakir fi masjid Dimashq: 1. Fi dhamm man la ya'mal bi-'ilmih, 2. Fi dhamm qurana' al-su'.* Ed. M. M. al-Hafiz. Damascus: Dar al-Fikr, 1979, pp. 29–42.

Majlis 19: *Fi tahrim al-ubna.* Ms. Zahiriyya *majmu'* 9, ff. 165–167.

Majlis 32: *Fi al-tawba.* In *Majmu' fih: 1. al-Tawba, 2. Hadith ahl Hurdan, 3. Dhamm dhu al-wajhayn wa-l-lisanayn, 4. Fadl shahr Ramadan, 5. Fadl yawm 'Arafa.* Ed. M. al-Mityari. Beirut: Dar Ibn Hazm, 2001, pp. 29–52

Majlis 45: *Fi madh al-tawadu' wa-dhamm al-kibar.* Ed. M. 'A-R al-Nabulusi. Damascus: Dar al-Sanabil, 1993.

Majlis 46: *Fi fadl 'A'isha.* Ed. H. al-Haddadi. Beirut: Dar al-Basha'ir, 2005.

Majlis 47: *Fi fadl Sha'ban.* Ms. Zahiriyya *majmu'* 98, ff. 98–106.

Majlis 51: *Fi fadl al-sawm.* Ms. Zahiriyya *majmu'* 20, ff. 103–108.

Majlis 52: *Fi dhamm al-malahi.* Ed. 'A. D. al-Firyati. Beirut: Dar al-Basha'ir, 2005.

Majlis 53: *Fi dhamm qurana' al-Su'.* In *Majlisan min majalis al-hafiz Ibn 'Asakir fi masjid Dimashq: 1. Fi dhamm man la ya'mal bi-'ilmih, 2. Fi dhamm qurana' al-su'.* Ed. M. M. al-Hafiz. Damascus: Dar al-Fikr, 1979, pp. 43–57.

Majlis 101–123: *Kashf al-mughatta fi fadl al-Muwatta.* Ed. M. M. al-Hafiz. Damascus: Dar al-Fikr, 1992.

Majlis 127: *Fi dhamm dhi al-wajhayn wa-l-lisanayn.* In *Majmu' fih: 1. al-Tawba, 2. Hadith ahl Hurdan, 3. Dhamm dhu al-wajhayn wa-l-lisanayn, 4. Fadl shahr Ramadan, 5. Fadl yawm 'Arafa.* Ed. M. al-Mityari. Beirut: Dar Ibn Hazm, 2001, pp. 91–115.

Majlis 137: *Fi si'at rahmat Allah.* In *Thalathat Majalis li-Ibn 'Asakir: 1. Si'at Rahmat Allah ta'ala, 2. Nafi al-tashbih, 3. Sifat Allah ta'ala.* Ed. 'A. al-Kayyali. Dubai: Matba'at al-Bayan, 1996, pp. 35–62.

Majlis 138: *Fi nafi al-tashbih.* Ed. M. 'A. al-Hamadani. Amman: Dar al-Fath, 2013.

Majlis 139: *Fi sifat Allah ta'ala.* In *Thalathat Majalis li-Ibn 'Asakir: 1. Si'at Rahmat Allah ta'ala, 2. Nafi al-tashbih, 3. Sifat Allah ta'ala.* Ed. 'A. al-Kayyali. Dubai: Matba'at al-Bayan, 1996, pp. 87–113.

Majlis 221–222: *Fi fadl 'Ali b. Abi Talib.* Ed. Kh. Al-Sharif. *Majallat Majma' al-Lugha al-'Arabiyya bi-Dimashq* 81/1 (2006): 77–100.

Majlis 238: *Fi fadl Sa'd b. Abi Waqqas.* Ed. S. al-Shihabi. *Majallat al-Turath al-'Arabi* 11–12 (1983): 187–196.

Majlis 280: Fi fadl 'Abd Allah Ibn Mas'ud. Ed. S. al-Shihabi. Majallat Majma'
al-Lugha al-'Arabiyya bi-Dimashq 58/4 (1983): 753–771.

Majlis 366–367: Fi fadl Rajab. In Ada' ma wajab min bayan wad' al-wadda'in fi Rajab.
Ed. J. 'Azzun. Beirut: Mu'assasat al-Rayyan, 2000, pp. 301–320.

Majlis 405: Fi fadl Ramadan. In Majmu' fih: 1. al-Tawba, 2. Hadith ahl Hurdan,
3. Dhamm dhu al-wajhayn wa-l-lisanayn, 4. Fadl shahr Ramadan, 5. Fadl yawm
'Arafa. Ed. M. al-Mityari. Beirut: Dar Ibn Hazm, 2001, pp. 117–139.

Majlis: Fadilat dhikr Allah. Ms. Zahiriyya majmu' 24, ff. 92–97.

Majlis: Fi fadl yawm 'Arafa. In Majmu' fih: 1. al-Tawba, 2. Hadith ahl
Hurdan, 3. Dhamm dhu al-wajhayn wa-l-lisanayn, 4. Fadl shahr Ramadan, 5.
Fadl yawm 'Arafa. Ed. M. al-Mityari. Beirut: Dar Ibn Hazm, 2001, pp.
141–167.

Majlis: Fi hifz al-qur'an. Ed. Kh. Al-Sharif. Damascus: Dar al-Fara'id, 1996.

Majlis: Hadith Ahl Hurdan. In Majmu' fih: 1. al-Tawba, 2. Hadith ahl Hurdan, 3.
Dhamm dhu al-wajhayn wa-l-lisanayn, 4. Fadl shahr Ramadan, 5. Fadl yawm
'Arafa. Ed. M. al-Mityari. Beirut: Dar Ibn Hazm, 2001, pp. 53–89.

Classical Sources

Abu Shama (d. 665/1268). Dhayl 'ala al-Rawdatayn. Ed. M. Z. al-Kawthari.
Beirut: Dar al-Jil, 1974.

———. Al-Rawdatayn fi akhbar al-dawlatayn al-nuriyya wa-l-salahiyya. 4 vols. Ed.
I. al-Zaybaq. Beirut: Mu'assasat al-Risala, 1997.

'Alam al-Din al-Birzali (d. 739/1339). Al-Muqtafi 'ala Dhayl al-Rawdatayn. 4
vols. Ed. 'U. Tadmuri. Sayda: al-Maktaba al-'Asriyya, 2006.

Al-Badri (d. 894/1489). Nuzhat al-anam fi mahasin al-Sham. Ed. I. Salih.
Damascus: Dar al-Basha'ir, 2006.

Al-Bitar (d. 1335/1917). Hilyat al-Bashar fi tarikh al-qarn al-thalith 'ashar. 3 vols.
Ed. M. B. al-Bitar. Beirut: Dar Sadir, 1993.

Al-Burini (d. 1024/1615). Tarajim al-a'yan min abna' al-zaman. 2 vols. Ed. S.
al-Munajjid. Damascus: Matba'at al-Majma' al-'Ilmi al-'Arabi bi-Dimashq,
1959–1963.

Al-Dhahabi (d. 748/1348). Ta'rikh al-islam. 47 vols. Ed. 'U. Tadmuri. Beirut:
Dar al-Kitab al-'Arabi, 1987–1998.

———. Siyar a'lam al-nubala'. 28 vols. Eds Sh. al-Arna'ut et al. Beirut: Mu'assasat
al-Risala, 1996.

Al-Ghazzi (d. 1061/1651). Al-Kawakib al-sa'ira bi-a'yan al-mi'a al-'ashira. 3 vols.
Ed. J. S. Jabbur. Beirut: Dar al-Afaq al-Jadida, 1979.

Ibn 'Abd al-Hadi (d. 909/1503). Jam' al-juyush wa-l-dasakir 'ala Ibn 'Asakir. Ed.
M. F. Sa'd. Medina: al-Jami'a al-Islamiyya, 1996.

Ibn Abu Ya'la al-Farra' (d. 526/1131). *Tabaqat al-hanabila*. 2 vols. Ed. M. H. al-Faqi. Beirut: Dar al-Ma'rifa, n.d.

Ibn al-'Adim (660/1262). *Bughyat al-talab fi ta'rikh Halab*. 12 vols. Ed. S. Zakkar. Damascus: Dar al-Fikr, 1988.

Ibn al-Athir (d. 630/1233). *Al-Ta'rikh al-bahir fi al-dawla al-atabikiyya*. 10 vols. Ed. 'A.-Q. Talimat. Cairo: Dar al-Kutub al-Haditha, 1963.

Ibn Kathir (d. 774/1373). *Tabaqat al-fuqaha' al-shafi'iyyin*. Ed. A. al-Baz. Mansura: Dar al-Wafa', 2004.

Ibn Muhanna al-Khawlani (d. c. 370/980). *Ta'rikh Darayya wa-man nazal biha min al-sahaba wa-l-tabi'in wa-tabi'i al-tabi'in*. Ed. S. al-Afghani. Damascus: Matba'at al-Taraqqi, 1950.

Ibn Rafi' (d. 774/1372). *Al-Wafayat*. 2 vols. Eds S. M. 'Abbas and B. 'A. Ma'ruf. Beirut: Mu'assasat al-Risala, 1982.

Ibn Shaddad (d. 684/1285). *Al-A'laq al-khatira fi dhikr al-Sham wa-l-Jazira*. 3 vols. Ed. S. al-Dahhan et al. Damascus: Institut Français de Damas and Wizarat al-Thaqafa, 1953–1978.

Ibn Tulun (d. 953/1546). *Dhakha'ir al-qasr fi tarajim nubala' al-'asr*. 2 vols. Ed. N. M. al-Jilani. Amman: Dar Zahran, 2014.

'Imad al-Din al-Isfahani (597/1201). *Kharidat al-qasr wa-jaridat al-'asr: Qism Shu'ara' al-Sham*. 4 vols. Ed. Sh. Faysal. Damascus: al-Matba'a al-Hashimi-yya, 1955–1968.

Al-Mizzi (d. 742/1341). *Tahdhib al-Kamal fi asma' al-rijal*. 35 vols. Ed. B. Ma'ruf. Beirut: Mu'assasat al-Risala, 1980–1992.

Al-Muhibbi (d. 1111/1699). *Khulasat al-athar fi a'yan al-qarn al-hadi 'ashar*. 4 vols. Beirut: Dar Sadir, n.d.

Al-Muradi (d. 1206/1791). *Silk al-durar fi a'yan al-qarn al-thani 'ashar*. 4 vols. Beirut: Dar al-Basha'ir al-Islamiyya, 1988.

Al-Sakhawi (d. 902/1497). *Al-I'lan bi-l-tawbikh li-man dhamm al-tarikh*. Ed. F. Rosenthal. Baghdad: Maktabat al-Muthanna, 1963.

Al-Subki (d. 771/1370). *Tabaqat al-shafi'iyya al-kubra*. 6 vols. Ed. M. 'Ata. Beirut: Dar al-Kutub al-'Ilmiyya, 1999.

Yaqut al-Hamawi (d. 626/1229). *Mu'jam al-udaba'*. 7 vols. Ed. I. 'Abbas. Beirut: Dar al-Gharb al-Islami, 1993.

Modern Sources

Anderson, Benedict. *Imagined Communities: Reflections on the Origin and Spread of Nationalism*. London: Verso, 2016.

Antrim, Zayde. "Ibn 'Asakir's Representations of Syria and Damascus in the introduction to the *Ta'rikh madinat Dimashq*." *International Journal of Middle East Studies* 38/1 (2006): 109–129.

——. *Routes and Realms: The Power of Place in the Early Muslim World.* New York: Oxford University Press, 2012.

——. "Nostalgia for the Future: A Comparison between the Introductions to Ibn 'Asakir's *Ta'rikh madinat Dimashq* and al-Khatib al-Baghdadi's *Ta'rikh Baghdad.*" In *New Perspectives on Ibn 'Asakir in Islamic Historiography.* Eds. S. Judd and J. Scheiner. Leiden: Brill, 2017, pp. 9–29.

Chamberlain, Michael. *Knowledge and Social Practice in Medieval Damascus, 1190–1350.* Cambridge: Cambridge University Press, 1994.

Cobb, Paul M. "Community versus Contention: Ibn 'Asakir and 'Abbasid Syria." In *Ibn 'Asakir and Early Islamic History.* Ed. J. E. Lindsay. Princeton: Darwin Press, 2001, pp. 100–126.

Al-Dahhan, Sami. *Muhammad Kurd 'Ali: Hayatuh wa-atharuh.* Damascus: Arabic Academy of Science, 1955.

Dahman, Muhammad Ahmad. *Jabal Qasyun: bahth tarikhi tarif 'an hadha al-jabal.* Damascus: Matba't al-Taraqqi, 1946.

Donner, Fred M. "'Uthman and the Rashidun Caliphs in Ibn 'Asakir's *Ta'rikh madinat Dimashq*: A Study in Strategies of Compilation." In *Ibn 'Asakir and Early Islamic History.* Ed. J. E. Lindsay. Princeton: Darwin Press, 2001, pp. 44–61.

Écochard, Michel and Claude Le Cœur. *Les bains de Damas: monographies architecturales.* Damascus: Institut Français de Damas, 1942–1943.

Elisséeff, Nikita. *La description de Damas d'Ibn 'Asakir.* Damascus: Institut Français de Damas, 1959.

——. *Nur ad-Din: Un grand prince musulman de Syrie au temps des croisades (511–569 H./1118–1174).* 3 vols. Damascus: Institut Français de Damas, 1967.

Goudie, Kenneth A. *Reinventing Jihad: Jihad Ideology from the Conquest of Jerusalem to the End of the Ayyubids (c. 492/1099–647/1249).* Leiden: Brill, 2019.

Al-Hafiz, Muhammad Muti'. *Al-Hafiz Ibn 'Asakir: muhaddith al-Sham wa-mu'arrikhuha al-kabir, 499–571 H.* Damascus: Dar al-Qalam, 2003.

——. *Al-Mahasin al-sultaniyya fi Dar al-Hadith al-Nuriyya.* Damascus: Dar al-Bayruti, 2006.

Halwani, Ahmad. *Ibn 'Asakir wa-dawruh fi al-jihad didd al-salibiyyin fi 'ahd al-dawlatayn al-nuriyya wa-l-ayyubiyya.* Damascus: Dar al-Fida', 1991.

Hirschler, Konrad. *The Written Word in the Medieval Arabic Lands: A Social and Cultural History of Reading Practices.* Edinburgh: Edinburgh University Press, 2013.

——. *Medieval Damascus: Plurality and Diversity in an Arabic Library — The Ashrafiya Library Catalogue.* Edinburgh: Edinburgh University Press, 2016.

——. *A Monument to Medieval Syrian Book Culture: The Library of Ibn 'Abd al-Hadi.* Edinburgh: Edinburgh University Press, 2020.

Hobsbawm, Eric. *Nations and Nationalism since 1780: Programme, Myth, Reality.* Cambridge: Cambridge University Press, 1990.

Humphreys, R. Stephen. "Women as Patrons of Religious Architecture in Ayyubid Syria." *Muqarnass: An Annual on Islamic Art and Architecture* 11 (1994): 35–54.

Al-Husni, Muhammad Adib. *Kitab Muntakhab al-tawarikh li-Dimashq*. 3 vols. Intr. K. S. Salibi. Beirut: Dar al-Afaq al-Jadida, 1979.

Al-'Ishsh, Yusuf. *Fahras makhtutat Dar al-Kutub al-Zahiriyya: al-tarikh wa-mulhaqatih*. Damascus: Matba'at Dimashq, 1947.

Johnson, Nels. *Islam and the Politics of Meaning in Palestinian Nationalism*. London: Kegan Paul, 1982.

Judd, Steven. "Ibn 'Asakir's Peculiar Biography of Khalid al-Qasri." In *New Perspectives on Ibn 'Asakir in Islamic Historiography*. Eds S. Judd and J. Scheiner. Leiden: Brill, 2017, pp. 139–155.

Judd, Steven and Jens Scheiner, eds. *New Perspectives on Ibn 'Asakir in Islamic Historiography*. Leiden: Brill, 2017.

Khalek, Nancy. *Damascus after the Muslim Conquest: Text and Image in Early Islam*. New York: Oxford University Press, 2011.

———. "The Publication of the Dar al-Fikr Edition of Ibn 'Asakir's *Ta'rikh madinat Dimashq*." In *New Perspectives on Ibn 'Asakir in Islamic Historiography*. Eds S. Judd and J. Scheiner. Leiden: Brill, 2017, pp. 4–8.

Khalidi, Rashid. "Arab Nationalism in Syria: The Formative Years, 1908–1914." In *Nationalism in a Non-National State: The Dissolution of the Ottoman Empire*. Eds W. W. Haddad and W. Ochsenwald. Columbus: Ohio State University Press, 1977, pp. 207–238.

———. "Society and Ideology in Late Ottoman Syria." In *Problems of the Modern Middle East in Historical Perspective: Essays in Honour of Albert Hourani*. Ed. J. P. Spagnolo. Reading: Ithaca Press, 1992, pp. 119–131.

Al-Khatib al-Hasani, Muhammad. *Dar al-Sunna: Dar al-Hadith al-Nuriyya bi-Dimashq, wa-tarikhuha wa-tarajim shuyukhiha*. Ed. M. M. al-Khatib al-Hasani. Damascus: Dar al-Basha'ir, 2002.

Khoury, Philip S. *Urban Notables and Arab Nationalism*: The Politics of Damascus, 1860–1920. Cambridge: Cambridge University Press, 1983.

Köhler, Michael A. *Alliances and Treatises between Frankish and Muslim Rulers in the Middle East: Cross Cultural Diplomacy in the Period of the Crusades*. Trans. P. M. Holt. Revised, ed. and intr. K. Hirschler. Leiden: Brill, 2013.

Kramer, Martin. *Arab Awakening & Islamic Revival: The Politics of Ideas in the Middle East*. New Brunswick: Transaction Publishers, 1996.

Kurd 'Ali, Muhammad. *Kitab Khitat al-Sham*. 6 vols. Damascus: al-Matba'a al-Haditha, 1925–1928.

———. *Al-Islam wa-l-hadara al-'Arabiyya*. Cairo: Dar al-Kutub al-Misriyya, 1934–1936.

——. *Al-Mudhakkarat*. Damascus: Matba'at al-Taraqqi, 1948–1951.

——. *Ghutat Dimashq*. Damascus: Matba'at al-Taraqqi, 1949 (first edition), 1952 (second improved edition).

——. *Kunuz al-ajdad*. Damascus: Matba'at Dimashq, 1950.

Lindsay. James E. "Damascene Scholars during the Fatimid Period: An Examination of 'Ali b. 'Asakir's *Ta'rikh Madinat Dimashq*." *Al-Masaq* 7 (1994): 35–75.

——. "'Ali Ibn 'Asakir as a Preserver of *Qisas al-Anbiya*': The Case of David ibn Jesse." *Studia Islamica* 82 (1995): 45–82.

——. "Caliphal and Moral Exemplar? 'Ali Ibn 'Asakir's Portrait of Yazid ibn Mu'awiya." *Der Islam* 74 (1997): 250–278.

——, ed. *Ibn 'Asakir and Early Islamic History*. Princeton: Darwin Press, 2001.

——. "Sarah and Hagar in Ibn 'Asakir's *Ta'rikh madinat Dimashq*." *Medieval Encounters: Jewish, Christian and Muslim Culture in Confluence and Dialogue* 10 (2008): 1–14.

McCarthy, Richard J. *The Theology of al-Ash'ari*. Beirut: Imprimerie Catholique, 1953.

Mehren, August Ferdinand. *Exposé de la réforme de l'islamisme commencée au IIIème siècle de l'Hégire par Abou-'l-Hasan Ali el-Ash'ari et continuée par son école avec des extraits du texte arabe d'Ibn Asâkir*. Leiden: Brill, 1878.

Mourad, Suleiman A. "Jesus according to Ibn 'Asakir." In *Ibn 'Asakir and Early Islamic History*. Ed. J. E. Lindsay. Princeton: The Darwin Press, 2001, pp. 24–43.

——. "Publication History of *Ta'rikh madinat Dimashq* (The History of Damascus)." In *Ibn 'Asakir and Early Islamic History*. Ed. J. E. Lindsay. Princeton: The Darwin Press, 2001, pp. 127–133.

——. "Jihad Propaganda in Early Crusader Syria: A Preliminary Examination of the Role of Displaced Scholars in Damascus." *Al-'Usur al-Wustta: Bulletin of Middle East Medievalists* 20.1 (2008): 1–7.

——. "A Critique of the Scholarly Outlook of the Crusades: The Case for Tolerance and Coexistence." In *Syria in Crusader Times: Conflict and Coexistence*. Ed. C. Hillenbrand. Edinburgh: Edinburgh University Press, 2020, pp. 144–160.

Mourad, Suleiman A. and James E. Lindsay. *The Intensification and Reorientation of Sunni Jihad Ideology in the Crusader Period: Ibn 'Asakir (1105–1176) of Damascus and His Age; with an edition and translation of Ibn 'Asakir's* The Forty Hadiths for Inciting Jihad. Leiden: Brill, 2013.

Al-Munajjid, Salah al-Din. *Khitat Dimashq: nusus wa-dirasat fi tarikh Dimashq al-tu-pugraphy wa-athariha al-qadima*. Beirut: Catholic Press, 1949.

Riley-Smith, Jonathan. *The Crusades, Christianity, and Islam*. New York: Columbia University Press, 2008.

Sajdi, Dana. Ibn 'Asakir's Children: Monumental Representations of Damascus until the 12th/18th Century." In *New Perspectives on Ibn 'Asakir in Islamic Historiography*. Eds S. Judd and J. Scheiner. Leiden: Brill, 2017, pp. 30–63.

Salibi, Kamal S. *Syria under Islam: Empire on Trial, 634–1097.* Delmar: Caravan Books, 1977.

Scheiner, Jens. "Ibn 'Asakir's Virtual Library as Reflected in his *Ta'rikh madinat Dimashq.*" In *New Perspectives on Ibn 'Asakir in Islamic Historiography*. Eds S. Judd and J. Scheiner. Leiden: Brill, 2017, pp. 156–257.

Al-Shihabi, Qutayba. *Mu'jam Dimashq al-tarikhi.* 3 vols. Damascus: Wizarat al-Thaqafa, 1999.

Shumaysani, Hasan. *Al-Hafiz Ibn 'Asakir.* Beirut: Dar al-Kutub al-'Ilmiyya, 1990.

Syrian Ministry of Higher Education. *Ibn 'Asakir: al-Kalimat wa-l-buhuth wa-l-qasa'id al-mulqat fi al-ihtifal bi-mu'arrikh dimashq al-kabir fi dhikra murur tis'uma'at sana 'ala wiladatih 499–1399 H.* Damascus: Ministry of Higher Education, 1979.

Tabbaa, Yasser. "Monuments with a Message: Propagation of *Jihad* under Nur al-Din." In *The Meeting of Two Worlds: Cultural Exchange between East and West during the Period of the Crusades.* Ed. V. P. Goss. Kalamazoo: Medieval Institute Publications, 1986, pp. 223–240.

White, Hayden. *The Content of the Form: Narrative Discourse and Historical Representation.* Baltimore: Johns Hopkins University Press, 1987.

Winet, Monika. "Female Presence in Biographical Dictionaries: Ibn 'Asakir's Selection Criteria for Women in his *Ta'rikh madinat Dimashq.*" In *New Perspectives on Ibn 'Asakir in Islamic Historiography*. Eds S. Judd and J. Scheiner. Leiden: Brill, 2017, pp. 93–138.

Zachs, Fruma. *The Making of Syrian Identity: Intellectuals and Merchants in Nineteenth Century Beirut.* Leiden: Brill, 2005.

INDEX